The Release of the Human Spirit

The Release of the Human Spirit

Frank Houston

Take note that the name satan and related names are not capitalized. We choose not to acknowledge him, even to the point of violating grammatical rules.

Destiny Image® Publishers, Inc.
P.O. Box 310
Shippensburg, PA 17257-0310

"Speaking to the Purposes of God for This Generation
and for the Generations to Come"

ISBN 0-7684-2019-9

For Worldwide Distribution
Printed in the U.S.A.

First Printing: 1999 Second Printing: 1999

Dedication

To my precious wife, Hazel, who has been my constant companion and wisest adviser for 50 years.

Also to our five wonderful children and their spouses: Maureen and David Bradshaw, Graeme and Carolyn Houston, Brian and Bobbie Houston, Beverley and Marcus Stacey, and Judith and Stephen McGhie.

Acknowledgments

Special thanks to the publishers, Destiny Image Publishers, Inc.; in particular Don Nori, Don Milam, Jeff Hall, and Steve Nance.

Endorsements

"The bindings on this book cover must be extra strong! That's the only thing I know that keeps this book from 'exploding'! Veteran warrior Frank Houston weakens the walls that confine and contain me. He helps me to 'break out' of the basement of negativity. If there's a sound barrier, then there could be a 'faith' barrier! Frank Houston breaks the 'faith' barrier in this book, *The Release of the Human Spirit*. He takes the elevator of faith to floors of God's promises that most of us miss. Are you ready to release your spirit? To go to the next level? Frank pushes the button labeled 'the sky's the limit' as we leave legalism, illness, and poverty below! Suddenly we 'break out' of barrenness and 'break through' the false glass ceiling and believe that 'all things are possible'! Change is in the air! Going up? Thank you, Frank, for your elevator of faith."

–Tommy Tenney
Evangelist and Revivalist
Author of *The God Chasers*

"The Bible tells us that there are not many fathers among us. Frank Houston is a father to a generation of young men and women. Pastor Frank's latest book will unlock and release your spirit to fulfill God's purpose for your life. If there is one man who has released people and helped them to break out, it is Pastor Frank Houston.

This book is a must. Read it. Then read it again, and more importantly, do what Pastor Franks says!"

—Pat Mesiti
Evangelist/Pastor
Hills Christian Life Centre, Sydney, Australia

"How is it that a Christian leader well past 75 years old can be more active, more visionary, more effective, and more dynamic than a man half his age? Frank Houston, one of the true fathers of the modern Pentecostal movement in Australia, lets you in on the keys that have kept him from spiritual stagnation and allowed him to grow and flow with each fresh move of God. Isn't it time for you to break out too?"

—Dr. Michael L. Brown
President
Brownsville Revival School of Ministry

"Whoever reads this book with an open mind and heart will be both challenged and refreshed. Frank Houston's message on breakout or containment is absolutely inspired! This teaching is essential for both leader and lay person alike. I highly recommend it."

—Bayless Conley
Senior Pastor
Cottonwood Christian Center

"Frank Houston has been a father in the faith for many years. He has a wealth of experience gained from decades of ministry. He is a role model for young preachers, and his passion for souls and his love for the saints are evident in this challenging book."

—Ray McCauley
Pastor
Randberg, South Africa

"Frank Houston is a very able communicator who passes on a wealth of insights based on more than 50 years of life and ministry.

Frank gives much needed keys to 'breaking out' into successful Christian living."

—John Arnott
Senior Pastor
Toronto Airport Christian Fellowship

"Having grown up in the home of Frank Houston, I have first-hand knowledge of the way he lives his life. This book captures the heartbeat and spirit of the man who has had the greatest influence and impact on my life. Through him, I have learned how to change my mind-set, go beyond the boundaries of tradition, and dream big dreams. It's what he has done all his life: taking God at His Word, expecting the miraculous, and having the courage to step out when nobody else was. He has lived an exceptional life in striving to reach his maximum potential and, as a result, has seen the purposes of God come to pass. You cannot read this book and settle for any less than the best for your life. It reveals the powerful truths and principles that will challenge your thinking and launch you into your God-given destiny. Once you've read it, anything can happen—and it probably will!"

—Brian Houston
President of Hillsongs Australia
National Superintendent of Assemblies of God in Australia

Contents

Foreword

Frank Houston is one of the Body of Christ's all-time giants in God. His long list of ministry experience ranges from working with the Salvation Army to being general superintendent of the Assemblies of God. Even after that, he went to a different country and planted a new church—a church that in turn has planted numerous other churches throughout the nation. What is most amazing is that he did that church planting in his 50's! To him age is no barrier!

Frank's book, *The Release of the Human Spirit*, shares the principles of revival that he has lived by for more than 50 years. It will bless, encourage, and motivate you to receive more from the Father in ways that you never before imagined. You, too, can "break out" from what contains and stifles you into a new and glorious freedom!

Ken and Lois Gott
Revival Now! International Ministries
Sunderland, England

Chapter 1

Containment or Breakout?

It was a critical moment for me as a Christian minister. I was driving through a suburb in one of three lanes of traffic when all of a sudden another car cut across my lane, causing me to slam on my brakes. The young man in the other car promptly sped off toward the traffic lights in the distance. I was just recovering from some health problems that had required me to spend several months in hospitals, and I was discouraged, depressed, and on the verge of backsliding. Now, the inconsiderate driver had left me angry, fuming mad even. I sped off also, hoping to catch up with him and really give him a piece of my mind.

I was pleased to see that the traffic light had turned red as I pulled up next to him. If it had been green I would have missed my opportunity. The other driver had his window open, so I cranked mine down and let him have it.

"Just where do you think you are going?" I shouted.

Flashing me a big, warm smile the young man said simply, "Home!"

At that simple, sincere answer, something broke inside of me and I burst out laughing. I hadn't laughed for days; perhaps even weeks. A few moments later the light changed to green, the young man waved, I waved back, and off we went. I laughed for at least two miles. I couldn't stop. Every time I tried, I would think about that smile and that single, simple word, and break out laughing again. I felt in my spirit that the young man was a Christian. To this day I am sure that he was a believer. His face was absolutely radiant. Although that event happened quite a number of years ago, I have never forgotten it.

That day, through a single word from a believer, God broke me out of the restricting container that I had allowed the negative circumstances of my life to squeeze me into. The same thing happened to the apostle Peter. At a single word from Jesus, Peter stepped out of the boat and walked on the water (see Mt. 14:28-29). Yes, he began to sink shortly thereafter and was rescued by Jesus, but Peter's experience lifted him to a higher plane of living. His attitude changed and he was saved from a limiting mind-set that threatened to prevent him from moving forward into everything that God wanted for him.

Containment

My encounter with the young motorist at the traffic light that day did the same thing for me. Until then, I was restricted and hemmed in all around by the discouragement of my recent illness and a basically negative frame of mind. This negativity influenced everything I said, did, or thought at home, church, or anywhere else at that time. I was in a state of containment that prevented me from rising above and moving beyond the immediate circumstances of my life.

> Containment is one of satan's most powerful and effective strategies against Christians. It is successful because it is subtle.

Containment is one of satan's most powerful and effective strategies against Christians. As John Avanzinni says, "The devil is not concerned nearly as much with driving you backward as he is with containing you where you are and keeping you from getting where God wants you to go."[1] Containment is successful because it is subtle. Pushing us backward would be too obvious. Satan, crafty devil that he is, would rather lull us into a false sense of security; into a comfortable complacency safe from the challenges and excitement of breaking out into the fuller, deeper, and richer realities that God desires for us in every area of life. And why not? A contained Christian is an ineffective Christian. A contained Christian is a non-growing

1. John Avanzinni, *Financial Excellence: A Treasury of Wisdom and Inspiration* (Tulsa, OK: Harrison House, 1993), 9.

Christian. A contained church is an irrelevant church. A contained church is a dying church. Containment keeps us from reaching the lost with the gospel and from having a positive influence on our society and culture.

Do you see the enemy's strategy here? Satan does not need to destroy the Church in order to win. All he has to do is make us irrelevant and ineffective, unworthy of the world's attention. It is as if he puts an invisible wall around us and takes us out of the action. With the Church on the sidelines, satan wins by default.

Consider worship, for example. Every now and then in my church in Sydney, Australia, I observe the congregation in worship. No matter how exciting or uplifting or anointed the worship is, no matter how much the worship leaders lose themselves in worshiping God, no matter how full the room is with a sense of the presence of God, there are always some, sometimes many, who are not really joining in. They may respectfully bow their heads or mutter in some language, but there is something missing. There is no robust singing in the Spirit. There is no passionate praise. There is no breakthrough. People are contained in their worship, and nothing much is happening.

Just about any pastor anywhere in the world could tell a similar story because containment is a common problem. It occurs in every area of life and affects all of us at one time or another. For whatever reason, we get locked up; the devil surrounds us with a shell, as it were, saying, "Only so far and no farther."

The devil doesn't worry much about us as long as we are contained in meaningless ritual that does nothing for us and nothing for God. We are praying the same prayers every day, reading the same book of the Bible every day, and doing whatever it is we do for God every day. In truth, we are doing little harm to the kingdom of satan and even less good for the Kingdom of God...and that's the whole idea. But the moment we decide to be students of God's Word, intercessors, or active witnesses among our friends and neighbors, we have a battle on our hands.

I know from personal experience that whenever I decide to increase my prayer life, to go beyond the boundaries of where I am to new levels of prayer, I suddenly find myself bombarded with all sorts of spiritual conflict and warfare. Discordant thoughts of every kind flood my mind to stop me from moving forward. As long as I am contained where I am, the devil more or less lets me alone. The moment I start to break out of my container, however, he is right there to try and stop me.

The devil hates praying saints. He wages warfare against believers who take praise and intercession seriously. He initiates combat whenever any of us launch out in a way that threatens his domain. If I say that I am going to read more of God's Word, I can count on it that the enemy will erect an invisible wall to prevent me from doing what I have set out to do. All kinds of things happen to stop me from breaking out and doing something different.

I know that I am not alone. Satanic opposition always arises whenever any one of us chooses to do something that is going to take us beyond where we are. How often do you read and study the Bible? Daily? Once a week? Once a month? Almost never? Wherever you are, if you decide to change, to move to a higher level, to study the Word more for your own edification and the building up of your spiritual life, then get ready for the attack. The devil wants you to stay where you are.

That's precisely what containment is all about. By definition, containment is keeping someone or something within limits by restraining, controlling, checking, or halting.[2] That's exactly what the devil seeks to do. He tries to prevent us from doing anything that will cause us to move beyond where we now are.

Many, many Christians are being contained. They can't get out of satan's container. They are church people who go to church on Sundays and then go through the humdrum business of getting up at the same time every Monday morning and returning to the monotony of the week. As they get on the bus or climb into the car, they join other contained people who are doing the same things they do every Monday morning.

Have you ever seen anything so boring? In cars, buses, and commuter trains, people are sitting there bored out of their minds. Some may be reading a newspaper or a novel, and every now and then you may see a Christian who has broken out of the box and is reading his Bible, but for the most part people just sit there in silence, being bored and contained.

Satan likes bored, contained Christians. He resists those who try to move beyond the invisible walls he erects. These walls of containment may have held you back for years. It should not surprise you, then, that satan will use many a trick should you try to break out of

---

2. See *Merriam-Webster's Collegiate Dictionary*, 10th edition (Springfield, MA: Merriam-Webster, Incorporated, 1994), 249, contain.

your current mind-set or move beyond your present limitations. All sorts of doubts, questions, and distractions will come, and moving forward will be much harder than you ever expected. Indeed, satan will actively oppose you.

> **Satan likes bored, contained Christians; he actively opposes believers who try to move beyond the status quo.**

Containment is not limited to the spiritual areas of life. It also attacks your mind–indeed, your entire manner of living. You may be contained by what you think about yourself, your family, and other people. Or you may be contained in the material realm by your attitudes and practices regarding money and possessions. Fear is a cause of containment for millions of people. So are emotional hurts and problems of many kinds.

Every day satan seeks to contain you, to imprison you in a life of boredom, mediocrity, and insignificance. God's heart and desire for you, on the other hand, is that you experience *breakout living*–rising above the sameness of daily life and reaching beyond your present experience and circumstances to fulfill your potential and do what God has purposed you should do. Breakout living looks *forward* rather than backward, and *upward* rather than downward. The apostle Paul expressed a "breakout" approach to life when he wrote to the Philippians:

> *Brethren, I do not count myself to have apprehended; but one thing I do, forgetting those things which are behind and reaching forward to those things which are ahead, I press toward the goal for the prize of the upward call of God in Christ Jesus* (Philippians 3:13-14).

A Vision in the Night

I have been in the ministry for over 50 years: raised a Baptist; saved in the Salvation Army at the age of 18; served as a Salvation Army officer for 12 years; and after receiving the baptism of the Holy Spirit, immersed for 40 years and counting in the Pentecostal movement. During most of those years my ministry has been, at least subconsciously, a breakout ministry. This is true not because I made a deliberate decision, but because that is the type of person I am and that is where my anointing is.

The presence or absence of a breakout mind-set is quite evident in how we respond to life's situations. For many of the early years of my life I battled sickness and poor health to live a normal life and maintain an active, busy ministry. It's only been in the latter years of my life that I have been healthy, but my poor health didn't stop me from battling on and doing the work that God gave me to do. Indeed, that struggle produced in me a breakout philosophy toward life itself because I discovered early on in the Word that Jesus Christ was nailed to the cross not only for my sins but also for my sicknesses and diseases. With His stripes I am saved, forgiven, and *healed*. (See Isaiah 53:5.)

In fact, twice since I moved to Sydney, it looked like I was going to die. Twice. Once I nearly bled to death. (The doctors told me that my blood level was below the point where it becomes fatal.) Yet I will never forget the peace that just flooded over me as I lay in the hospital. I knew that I was not going to die. I had the blessed assurance that the same Spirit that had raised Jesus from the dead would quicken my mortal body, and He did. Hallelujah!

Then in 1993, it looked like I was going down the tubes again, and once more the Spirit of life quickened my mortal body. In the past 5 years, I've done more work than in the previous 15, and that's saying a lot because I did much work then.

Jesus, speaking to the Jews who had believed in Him, said, "If you abide in My word, you are My disciples indeed. And you shall know the truth, and the truth shall make you free" (John 8:31b-32a). Now notice, it is not the truth that makes you free. It is the truth *you know* that sets you free. God didn't promise me that I wouldn't get sick, but He did promise that He would heal me. I'm not looking for sickness; I'm looking for health...divine health. The truth of God's healing word has become revelation knowledge in me.

I remember well how God used the truth of His Word to set me free in 1990. I was desperately ill and people thought that I was going to die. Now, I read the Word every day, but at that time God spoke into my life very clearly and said, "Read the psalms every day. Start at Psalm 1 and read a psalm every night." So I started that very day.

That reading of God's Word–consecutively, one psalm after another–and of writing my observations–even though I wasn't really physically fit to do it–was the process God used to heal me. Some nights I wasn't well and my pen would run off the paper; then I'd wake up the next morning and finish my notes. Through my reading, beginning with Psalm 1 and continuing to the end, God strengthened me and raised me up. His Word, His truth made real in my heart, set me free. Glory! Hallelujah!

This is but one incident I could share with you. In truth, I have experienced the wonder of this reality throughout my life and have been healed of physical ailments on a number of occasions. This is true partly because early in my Pentecostal ministry I was blessed to be linked up with Ray Bloomfield, a man born out of time way back in those early days. Ray ministered widely all across New Zealand, doing great miracles and walking in amazing supernatural realms—levels where no one else in the southern hemisphere was walking at the time. God brought us together, and I worked alongside him for a couple of years in a church he was pioneering. He mentored me and I witnessed the amazing things God was doing in his ministry. I saw the power of knowing and acting on the truth of God's Word.

Building on this foundation, I established a pattern for breakout in my own ministry. Even in the early days I was a bit of a rebel. I was always trying to push into territory no one else had ever been in. So in one way or another, I have always been breaking out in my ministry.

Perhaps the defining moment for me came on a night in mid-January, 1977. I was 55 years old and in my eighteenth year of pastoring a growing church in Wellington, New Zealand. (I had also been the General Superintendent of the Assemblies of God churches in New Zealand for 14 years.) I was doing all right, working with people I loved, but so much of what I did was from habit or because it seemed like the thing to do. I had grown stale. I was contained and needed a challenge. God broke in on me and gave me the opportunity to move on.

My wife Hazel was away on a vacation at the time, so I was alone the night God gave me a vision of Sydney, Australia. It was quite vivid. As I sought to understand the vision, God spoke to my heart and told me to read Isaiah chapter 54. From 11:30 that night until the sun rose the following morning, I immersed myself in that chapter. God spoke to me out of every verse, helping me to understand that He was getting me on the move, breaking me out of the containment that I was in. I had a marvelous night propped up in bed, cross-referencing and studying that chapter while God spoke right into my heart.

In the early hours of the morning I said, "Lord, what's the bottom line? What are You telling me?" I felt the Holy Spirit say to me very clearly, "I want you to go to Sydney and plant a church." My first reaction was, "But Lord, I'm 55 years old!" The Lord said to me, "What has that got to do with it?" "Nothing!" I replied. (What do you say to God Almighty when He gives you a vision and speaks to you?) Then I simply said, "Yes, Lord, I'll go," and was flooded with an unbelievable peace.

It took six months to wind up all our affairs in Wellington. In July, 1977, we flew across the Tasman Sea and planted a church in Sydney. When I went to Sidney, there was nothing happening. Most churches had 100 or less in services on a Sunday morning.

So we started the first Sunday with nine adults and five children. In the 21 years since, over 70 new churches have been planted across Australia and in different parts of the world from our original congregation in Sydney, and the number grows every year. In 1998 alone we started new churches in Copenhagen, Denmark; Perth, Australia; and the United States. These are but a few of the 50 churches we determined in 1995 to start by the year 2000. Because we are ahead of our strategy, we will probably start more than 50 churches. Multitudes of lives have been changed, growing out of one decision to say yes to God.

Song of the Barren One

Twenty years have come and gone since the night of that vision, but Isaiah chapter 54 still speaks powerfully to me about God's people breaking out of containment. Consider the first verse:

> *"Sing, O barren, you who have not borne! Break forth into singing, and cry aloud, you who have not labored with child! For more are the children of the desolate than the children of the married woman," says the Lord* (Isaiah 54:1).

Or to say it another way, "Sing, O barren one, you who live a mediocre kind of existence within the walls of satan's boundaries. Sing, you who are not producing fruit. Break forth into singing and shout aloud." Now, some of you may be saying, "I can't shout. I'm a dignified soul." Don't you believe it! That's satan's lie. God wants you to break loose. He doesn't want you to be so dignified in the silence of your mediocrity and your pose of looking good. He calls you to enter in not because somebody tells you to, but because inwardly you have a genuine desire to worship Him and to be caught up into passionate service and heartfelt obedience to Him.

Others of you have little strength or heart to shout because your life has been everything but fruitful. One unfulfilled promise after another looms large on your horizon and you spend your days wishing for what might have been and fearing what yet may come.

Isaiah speaks poignantly into your situation. Can you imagine a better picture of hopelessness and containment than barrenness? The specific image portrayed here is of a woman who has borne no children–either because she is unable or because she has been forsaken, widowed, or abandoned–yet the meaning goes far beyond this to depict lifelessness, fruitlessness, and unfulfilled potential.

You may know all too well just what I am talking about. One job after another has come and gone, yet you are still bored and searching for meaning and purpose. Or perhaps you've been through two or three marriages, always hoping that you will find someone to love and be loved by for the rest of your life. Or yet again, you may have a journal filled with prophecies that the Lord's servants have spoken over you, prophecies that have yet to be accomplished in your life.

Don't give up, my friend. Break out. Give yourself with abandon to work and love and prayer. When things start to go wrong–and I guarantee they will when you start to break out–persevere in doing whatever God shows you to do. You'll soon discover the wonder of breaking into a whole new realm, a realm of love, power, and the blessings of Almighty God. Whether it's working at a boring job, loving the unlovely, or serving the Lord right where you are today, do so with unrestrained abandon–not because you have the power to change your circumstances, but because God does.

In the context of Isaiah chapter 54, the barren woman represents the nation of Israel. To the ancient Hebrews, barrenness was considered a curse from God. Yet, the barren woman is here told to "break forth into singing and cry aloud." In the original language, the words translated "sing," "singing," and "cry aloud" also mean to shout for joy or to shout in triumph. So the barren one is commanded to shout for joy, to give a victory cry. Why? The Lord is bringing about a reversal: The barren woman will now have more offspring than the "married woman." In other words, God is going to bring about breakout in the life of the barren woman. She will no longer be contained in her barren state.

When God spoke to me from Isaiah chapter 54 that January night in 1977, I understood the shout to mean a breaking of something within me; God was severing me from the past and giving me a new beginning. I had to obey Him even when it didn't seem to make sense from the standpoint of my human understanding. So when God told me to plant a church in Sydney, I shouted a "yes" of obedience. Six months later, when our family flew to Sydney, we had no home, no car, no meeting place–nothing. Yet God very quickly met us at every point of need. He answered our shout.

What has been true for me is also possible for you. Christ-like lives that present a positive witness of God's love, grace, and power are the mighty work of the Holy Spirit in this day and hour. He's taking us to realms we never dreamed of seeing and making us effective to change the world in our lifetime. So, if you are a lifeless, bored Christian who is contained, bearing little fruit, and showing little promise, it's time for you to be released into a whole new dimension of life–life filled with hope, expectation, spiritual power, and accomplishments beyond anything you have ever imagined. For your sake and for the sake of a lost and dying world, you must break out of the shell that contains you. Now is the time to release yourself into God, to break through the barriers that hold you back, and to removed the roadblocks that satan and his demons have built in your life.

Chapter 2

The Harvest of Breakout

God yearns for all His children to break out of their contained lives and their restricted modes of thinking. He waits for them to walk in obedience so that He can work the victory. Then He brings forth all that He has promised. This is revealed in Isaiah chapter 54 in an amazing way.

> *Enlarge the place of your tent, and let them stretch out the curtains of your dwellings; do not spare; lengthen your cords, and strengthen your stakes. For you shall expand to the right and to the left, and your descendants will inherit the nations, and make the desolate cities inhabited* (Isaiah 54:2-3).

Do you see what God is promising? He's talking about expansion. That's what lengthening cords, strengthening stakes, and spreading out is all about. Indeed, that is the basic theme of this entire chapter in Isaiah. God is talking about going out and getting beyond your present situation. This doesn't necessarily mean leaving your church, but it does speak of expanding your spiritual life and getting direction from God in your own spirit.

When I studied these verses that January night in 1977, I wondered what they meant for me. "Your descendants will inherit the nations." What a powerful and exciting promise! In particular, I wondered who was referred to in the word *them*: "And let *them* stretch out the curtains of your dwellings."

As God spoke into my heart, He told me that He was going to give me a harvest. Over the past 21 years I have seen that promise abundantly fulfilled in ways I could never have dreamed of at the time. I have reaped a harvest both right here in Sydney and around the world. By the grace of God, literally thousands of people who have been saved or discipled through this church are now preaching, witnessing, and serving the Lord.

This harvest has included my own children, and now also my grandchildren and great-grandchildren. I remember the day one of the kids in our church carved a map of Australia for me out of plywood, put Sydney on it, and wrote my name, Frank, across the continent. I remember another youngster who was just a kid riding a lawnmower when he told me that he was going to marry my daughter...and he has. Now I watch his son, my 15-year-old grandson, who was drastically changed by the power and anointing of God when he attended the revival in Pensacola, Florida.

I also remember my son Brian, when he was a kid, sitting and watching me preach, and saying one day that he was going to do what his daddy did. He's doing it. For a while he was an associate pastor at our church. Today, he and his wife Bobbie are the senior pastors of Hills Christian Life Centre here in Sydney. This church, founded in 1984, has become one of the largest churches in Australia, and is the home of Hillsongs Australia, which focuses on drawing the Body of Christ into worship.

My sons and daughters, their sons and daughters, and the spiritual sons and daughters whom I have introduced to Jesus and nurtured in the faith—as well as the many still to come—are the "them" who are stretching out the curtains of my "dwelling." They are the spiritual descendants of the promise of expansion that the Lord spoke to my heart back in 1977.

Steps of Obedience

I certainly had no concept then of the extent to which God would enlarge my tent. I could not foresee the magnitude of His faithfulness and mercy that have unfolded in my life. Yet, this is the way of our God. When He begins to tell us something about the destiny He has planned for our lives, He doesn't usually give us a detailed description up front. Most of the time all we have is a basic outline, or maybe only a tiny thought.

Consider Abram, for example. When God spoke to him to leave his home and country, he didn't tell Abram where he was going. He simply said, "Get out of your country, from your family and from your father's house, to a land that I will show you" (Gen. 12:1b). Then He gave Abram a wonderful promise: "I will make you a great nation; I will bless you and make your name great; and you shall be a blessing. I will bless those who bless you, and I will curse him who curses you; and in you all the families of the earth shall be blessed" (Gen. 12:2-3).

God called Abram to break out—to leave the containment of the life he had always known—and to embark on a spiritual journey at a higher level than he had ever been at before, one in which he was completely dependent upon God. Then He gave Abram a promise that sounds much like the promise the Lord gave me from Isaiah 54. He promised Abram enlargement and expansion if he would respond to God with obedience.

God deals with all His children in this way. He doesn't tell us everything up front because He wants us to learn to trust Him. Also, if we saw the entire picture from the start and knew just how large the expansion would ultimately be, we might become too overwhelmed even to make the attempt. So God often gives us just the basic information we need to begin to obey Him. Our part, then, is to take those first few steps of obedience. That's where breakout begins.

> The only way to fulfill your destiny is to take the first step...and the next and the next...as God leads.

Those initial steps of obedience vary from individual to individual, but they all demand a commitment of faith. God may require you, for example, to resign from your job and move to another town or country to attend a Bible college or school of ministry. Or He may direct you to turn down a promotion or seek part-time instead of full-time employment so that you have the time to serve a particular individual or ministry. Yet again, He may ask you to open your home to an unwed mother or an impoverished widow.

At first these steps of obedience may not seem to be all that significant; but as you do everything that the Lord commands you, you will move beyond the confinement of where you have been into the destiny He has planned for you. It is then that you will begin to see the fruit of your commitment.

This is precisely what the Holy Spirit wants to do in each of our lives. He is seeking to do a gracious, powerful, mighty, and glorious work in us, moving us beyond the borders of all we have ever dreamed possible and helping us to become effective in our lifetime to change our world by the grace of God. Part of this enlargement and expansion occurs as we recognize and assume our unique place in the Body of Christ.

Each of us has this specific, individual, very special place within Christ's Body, the Church. As we draw near to God, He reveals to us where we fit in, and the Holy Spirit anoints us to function precisely within that position. Then it is our responsibility to move into the position that God shows us and to function effectively there. This is possible as we take on the character of breakout people.

Breakout Character

The *decision* to break out is *yours*, and yours alone. It is a choice *you* must make, a choice that is determined by the attitude and character of your heart. I believe that God looks for three particular qualities to move you from mediocrity and living that reaps little or no fruit. These essential characteristics for breakout living are a hunger for God, a teachable spirit, and an attitude of humility toward God.

Hunger for God

Are you hungry for God? Does your spirit crave His presence and His Word the way a starving man craves food? Do you thirst for Him the way a man lost in the desert thirsts for water? Hunger for God should be your natural and continuous state if you are a believer. The Book of Psalms clearly expresses this craving:

> *As the deer pants for the water brooks, so pants my soul for You, O God. My soul thirsts for God, for the living God. When shall I come and appear before God?* (Psalm 42:1-2)
>
> *O God, You are my God; early will I seek You; my soul thirsts for You; my flesh longs for You in a dry and thirsty land where there is no water* (Psalm 63:1).
>
> *My soul longs, yes, even faints for the courts of the Lord; my heart and my flesh cry out for the living God* (Psalm 84:2).
>
> *I spread out my hands to You; my soul longs for You like a thirsty land* (Psalm 143:6).

Jesus said, "Blessed are those who hunger and thirst for righteousness, for they shall be filled" (Mt. 5:6). Another psalm states that God "satisfies the longing soul, and fills the hungry soul with goodness" (Ps. 107:9). Who does God satisfy? The boy or girl, man or woman, who longs for God and thirsts for righteousness. Those who hunger for God and seek after Him will be filled. This is His promise.

Just because you are hungry you can rest in the assurance that you will be filled; and the more of Him you have, the more you will want and receive. That's why you can be filled and hungry at the same time.

A Teachable Spirit

The second quality of a breakout Christian is teachableness. I want to be taught. I want to be taught by the Word, by the Holy Spirit, and by the great men and women of faith whom God has placed in my path.

You can't receive from the Lord if you don't have a teachable spirit. This means both that you admit there is much you don't know and that you show a willingness to learn. People who think they know it all never become very effective in working for the Kingdom of God.

Consider this wisdom from Proverbs:

> *My son, give attention to my words; incline your ear to my sayings. Do not let them depart from your eyes; keep them in the midst of your heart; for they are life to those who find them, and health to all their flesh* (Proverbs 4:20-22).

A teachable spirit opens you up to the truths of God, which are *life* and *health* to you. Then God can fill you as you *listen* to His voice ("incline your ear"), read His Word ("do not let [my words] depart from your eyes") and *learn* it thoroughly ("keep them in the midst of your heart").

King David wrote, "Show me Your ways, O Lord; teach me Your paths. Lead me in Your truth and teach me, for You are the God of my salvation; on You I wait all the day" (Ps. 25:4-5). Talk about a hungry soul! Talk about a teachable spirit! Talk about wanting to know God's ways! It is no wonder then that David was described as a man after God's own heart (see 1 Sam. 13:14; Acts 13:22).

Humility Toward God

The third characteristic of breakout living is humility before God. The Kingdom of Heaven belongs to the humble. Jesus made that clear when He said, "Blessed are the poor in spirit, for theirs is the kingdom of heaven" (Mt. 5:3).

Just what is humility? It's an attitude of the heart. It doesn't mean groveling in the dirt or wearing sackcloth and ashes, but showing reverence and honor to God. As believers, we can boldly approach God's throne of grace (see Heb. 4:16), but we should never do so flippantly or carelessly. We can be joyful in His presence, even while we remember that He is God and we are sinners saved by grace. That's where humility comes in.

I like what James says:

> *Humble yourselves [feeling very insignificant] in the presence of the Lord, and He will exalt you [He will lift you up and make your lives significant]* (James 4:10 AMP).

Who will exalt you when you humble yourself before the Lord? The Lord will. It is He who *exalts* (lifts up) the humble and *makes their lives significant*! In the light of God's truth, and in the light of the knowledge that satan can hammer you into mediocrity and hem you into irrelevance and ineffectiveness, please consider how significant *your* life is right now. Are you living in breakout every day, experiencing the joy and refreshing of the river of life flowing from God's throne? Are you moving forward and upward in the things of the Lord, enjoying His presence daily? Are you fulfilling your potential, becoming all that you can be in God? Or are you living in containment, being restrained and unable to reach beyond your past or your own sense of limitations?

It's Time to Change

Breakout living means change, and the devil hates change. He will do anything in his power to prevent it because it threatens his kingdom. He gets the jitters whenever you get on your knees or have a serious thought about God's Word. He gets nervous the moment you begin thinking about holiness and righteousness. And if you think about repentance, he goes into apoplexy!

However, the devil cannot keep you from breaking out if you are committed to moving out and up and are seeking God with a hungry, teachable, and humble heart. God has given His grace, His presence, the authority of His Word and His name, and the power of His Spirit to enable you to break out of the boxes that have contained you and to move forward and upward into new dimensions of spiritual life and growth. This "breakout living" blesses you with several very specific provisions from God.

Descendants

First, God promises to give you descendants, both physical and spiritual, who are blessed because of your faithfulness to follow the Lord's calling on your life. You pass on a legacy to all who follow you, be they your physical children or your spiritual ones.

> *"All your children shall be taught by the Lord, and great shall be the peace of your children....No weapon formed against you shall prosper, and every tongue which rises against you in judgment you shall condemn. This is the heritage of the servants of the Lord, and their righteousness is from Me," says the Lord* (Isaiah 54:13,17).

As I already mentioned in Chapter 1, I have seen this Scripture fulfilled in the lives of each of my children and am now seeing it in the lives of my grandchildren. The promise is inclusive. *All* our children will be taught by the Lord. *All* our children will experience great peace. *All* our children will be blessed by the Lord. Not some of them, not most of them, but *all* of them. The Hebrew word used in Isaiah 54:13 for "peace" is *shalom*, which could also be translated "prosperity": Great shall be the *prosperity* of your children.

Come on, parents. Believe this and receive it in your hearts. Some of your children may rebel, but they won't rebel forever because God Almighty has locked them into your prayers and to your faith and believing. Live Christ-like before them. Don't fight in front of them. Don't say stupid things to them, or call them stupid. Don't say anything that will demean or diminish them or prohibit them from achieving their full potential in the Lord. Live righteously before your children. Move beyond the boundaries of satan's containment and be a godly example for them. What you teach them will remain with them, even if they rebel and leave for a time. That's what the Bible teaches:

> *So shall My word be that goes forth from My mouth; it shall not return to Me void, but it shall accomplish what I please, and it shall prosper in the thing for which I sent it* (Isaiah 55:11).
>
> *Train up a child in the way he should go, and when he is old he will not depart from it* (Proverbs 22:6).

Those of you who do not have children of your own can still model these things for the children you do come into contact with, be they relatives, the children of friends, or children at church. Remember also that this applies to spiritual children as well–those who are younger in the faith than you are.

I have been quite blessed to see fruit produced by those whom I have birthed and nurtured in faith. For example, I remember one young policeman–he was only about 19 years old at the time of this story–from my church in New Zealand. He was gloriously saved in my church and as a new convert, he was so on fire for God that he wanted to be in everything.

Every August the young people from our church would go up to Mount Ruapehu to the snow. They would leave Friday night and arrive up on the mountain in the early hours of Saturday morning. Then they would spend all Saturday skiing or enjoying whatever else they did in the snow.

As it turned out, this young policeman went with them and didn't dress properly for the outing. He had on just fairly light clothing. When icy, cold rain began falling on the mountain, he got wet through. Then, that night, he journeyed home in those same wet, cold clothes. The result of this was that in a few days he was so crippled up with rheumatism in his joints that he could not move. He also had a high fever. His mother and father put up a bed in their living room, and there he lay, locked in bed.

I lived just around the corner from this family. The young man's mother, who was not a Christian, called me and said, "My son is in bed with rheumatic fever, and the doctor has ordered him to go to the hospital; but he won't go until Pastor Frank Houston comes to pray for him."

I said, "I'll come right now." So my wife and I went around the corner to visit this young man. There he lay. He could not even get out of bed to go to the toilet–he was that crippled up–and he was in serious pain. I started reading Scriptures about healings, and my wife stood beside the mother and tried to explain a few of the Scriptures to her. Finally I said to the young man, "I am going to anoint you with oil. Then I am going to lay my hand on you, and Jesus Christ, the Son of God, is going to raise you up off that bed." So I anointed him with oil and put my hand on his head.

The moment I touched him, the power of God crackled like lightning. As it went up and down his body—you could just about see this power, this healing anointing, this wonderful presence of the Spirit of the living God—he shook violently and started to shout at the top of his voice. His mother thought that he was going crazy. In answer to her, "What's going on?" I said, "This young man is being healed by the power of God. Wait and see." Then not only did he shake and shout, but he began to jump up and down on his back on the bed. Then he leaped off the bed and ran up and down the hallway, shouting, "Praise God! I'm healed! Praise God! I'm healed! Praise God! I'm healed!" With that healing came a mighty impartation of the Spirit of God that just changed his life. Today he is a pastor in New Zealand—a wonderful man of God, a mighty man of valor. Through his ministry I now have many more spiritual descendants.

Nations

Second, breakout living provides the means for God to accomplish His purposes on the earth. This is true not only in our lifetime but also in the generations of our descendants. God, in Isaiah 54, promises that our descendants—our children, grandchildren and great-grandchildren—will "inherit the nations" (Is. 54:3). My descendants (both spiritual and natural) are doing just that—and will continue to do so. Some have matured in our midst and are even now making their mark on the world to the glory of God. Others are not settled down enough yet to understand what life is really all about, but one day they too will walk in the purposes that God has specifically laid out for their lives, and they will inherit the nations. Indeed, there may well be kids in my church now right now who will become great men and women of God long after I'm in Heaven.

I have particularly had the joy of seeing my son Brian fulfill part of his destiny to inherit the nations. When Brian was a baby, I used to lay hands on him and pray, "God, make this boy grow to be a mighty man of God." God has been faithful to answer that prayer. A man of faith and vision, Brian has had the opportunity to influence the United States and other countries around the world through the medium of television. In November 1998, he was also given the opportunity to influence the nation of Australia when he was invited to be the speaker at the opening church service of the Australian Parliament.

Freedom From Shame

Third, those who choose breakout living also reap the blessing of freedom from shame as God banishes all the shameful things of the past and sweeps them away forever. What a blessing this is! Most of us (if not all of us) have some kind of a shameful past–things that we are not pleased about, things we don't even want to talk about! Notice what God says about these:

> *Do not fear, for you will not be ashamed; neither be disgraced, for you will not be put to shame; for you will forget the shame of your youth, and will not remember the reproach of your widowhood anymore* (Isaiah 54:4).

Transformation Through God's Intervention

Fourth, breakout people who have been disgraced will reap the blessing of God's transforming power in their circumstances by reason of God's intervention. Perhaps you have spent time in prison. If you are a breakout Christian, that's over. It's finished. A whole new relationship with God and others is yours because you have broken out of your old life patterns through the power of God and for His glory.

When Jesus established His Church, He said that the gates of hell would not prevail against it (see Mt. 16:18). He also testified that He came to destroy the works of the devil (see 1 Jn. 3:8) and to empower His Church to do the same in His name (see Jn. 14:12-13). No wonder satan works so hard to contain us! He trembles at the thought of the Church living in breakout; of Christians recognizing and claiming their full heritage in Christ, walking in the presence of God, and operating in the power of the Spirit. This heritage is given to all servants of the Lord, as well as to their descendants after them. As Isaiah 54:17 states:

> *"No weapon formed against you shall prosper, and every tongue which rises against you in judgment you shall condemn. This is the heritage of the servants of the Lord, and their righteousness is from Me," says the Lord* (Isaiah 54:17).

Please note the first word of this verse: no. No opposition against the people of God can last, no matter how strong and invincible is may appear to be. Only God knows the prosperity and success that can be yours when you trust Him and commit yourself to moving beyond your containment into the breakout living He wants for you. As long as you keep your eyes on Jesus and remain focused on your vision, the only thing that can stop you is yourself. This applies both to you and to those who come after you.

Accept the Challenge

I know that my descendants will prosper and inherit the nations. I see it now and am certain that it will continue. In part, this will happen because I was faithful in 1977 to answer the call of God to leave New Zealand and go to Australia. In large measure, however, the heritage passed on to me by my ancestors is also the legacy that my descendants–both physical and spiritual–will build upon. This legacy goes back into my childhood and even to the years before I was born.

My mother was a praying woman, and she taught me to pray. I can well remember the many times she told me to kneel at her knee and say the prayers she taught me as a child. My father, although he forsook God for many years of his life, originally came out to New Zealand to be a missionary, and I have been able to trace a minister of the gospel in every generation of the Houston clan back through the eleventh century. Some of them were bishops and high-up officials in the Church. Today that legacy continues in my son and in two of my grandsons, who are sure that they will be ministers of the gospel.

I could tell you much more about God's faithfulness in the lives of my natural and spiritual children. He has been so good. Even more, I want you to see His faithfulness in your life when you choose to recognize and break free of the boxes in which satan has contained you.

Perhaps you have a legacy to pass on to your children that has been handed down to you, but you've been sidetracked or you have yet to experience breakout living. Today's the day to make the change. Break away from all the mediocrity, sluggishness, and fear (this is one of satan's most effective containment tools) that are consuming your life and get out where the victory is. God is just waiting for you to choose to break out. That's all it takes: your choice to break out.

Once you've make that choicc, He will provide the power to do it. He'll bless you, anoint you, and give you victory again and again and again until every wall, barrier, and other form of bondage is removed from your life, and the heritage reserved for God's servants becomes evident in you and all those who follow you. Whatever area of life you are contained in–mental (mind), spiritual, emotional, or material (we will discuss all these later in more depth)–God is ready to set you free.

Then you will discover the wonder of a whole new realm of life, a whole new realm of miracles, a whole new realm of love, and a whole new realm of the blessings of Almighty God. You will not be able to believe all that God will do for you if you will only break out. *Today is the day* ***you*** *must make the choice to break out!*

Chapter 3

Beyond Mental Limitation

I was not particularly successful in school as a boy. Certainly, I was no "standout" student. Where academics were concerned, my teachers gave me the feeling that I was about as dumb as they come. In fact, at one point the headmaster of my school told me point-blank, "Houston, you're never going to amount to anything."

For a long time I believed him. Fortunately for me, God had other plans. My headmaster did not take into account what God can do with a boy suffering from low self-esteem. Through the Holy Spirit's presence in my life empowering and encouraging me, I discovered that I had possibilities that I hadn't dreamed about; that I had a brain and could think. After my school years I basically educated myself in spite of my headmaster's limiting assessment. I refused to be contained any longer by his negative words. Furthermore, the Holy Spirit's indwelling presence inspired me and gave my life great purpose and direction.

Today, I love to think. In fact, I love it so much that my wife bought me a "think chair." I sit there in the evenings doing creative thinking, lateral thinking, and all kinds of thinking simply to increase my mental capacity and agility.

I mention this to point out the danger we all face of being contained by the negative, limiting words and opinions of others, as well as by our own mental processes. Containment in our minds is one of the biggest problems we face because we live in a negative and demeaning world. When we focus on this world, the natural realm with all its limitations, rather than on God's supernatural realm where the only "limitation" is eternity, we become mentally contained. Our habits and patterns of thinking reveal minds that are too small to embrace the limitless possibilities that exist in truly Spirit-filled living.

One day when Jesus and His disciples were in a boat crossing the Sea of Galilee, Jesus was asleep in the stern when a powerful storm blew up. The disciples, seeing only the storm, feared for their lives and woke Jesus. He rebuked the storm and immediately there was complete calm. Then Jesus rebuked His disciples with the words, "Where is your faith?" (Lk. 8:25) Jesus saw through the storm to the peace beyond. He was not contained by mere human understanding of nature.

Breakout, whether in the mind or anywhere else, involves learning to think the way Jesus thinks; to see from His perspective and not depend on your own limited vision. In his first letter to the Corinthian church the apostle Paul contrasted "natural" unsaved people with "spiritual" born-again believers:

> *But the natural man does not receive the things of the Spirit of God, for they are foolishness to him; nor can he know them, because they are spiritually discerned. But he who is spiritual judges all things, yet he himself is rightly judged by no one. For "who has known the mind of the Lord that he may instruct Him?" But we have the mind of Christ* (1 Corinthians 2:14-16).

Although the focus of these verses is on spiritual discernment, the truth applies also to our thinking and mental processes. Paul says that as believers "we have the mind of Christ." This means that we should think like Him, talk like Him, and act like Him. With His mind in us there is no excuse for any of us not to experience "breakout thinking" as a matter of course.

Unfortunately, too many of us who have the mind of Christ often think and act as if we are still men and women of the world. That's containment. Containment thinking shows up in many ways. These include the limitations of impossibility thinking, narrow thinking, mediocre thinking, compartmentalized thinking, and boredom.

"It Can't Be Done!"

One of the most serious hindrances to breakout thinking is an impossibility mentality–the "it can't be done" syndrome. This point of view focuses on obstacles rather than opportunities; on problems rather than possibilities.

In chapter 14 of his Gospel, Matthew relates a remarkable story that shows how Jesus dealt with an impossibility mentality. It is a wonderful lesson on breakout:

> *When Jesus heard it, He departed from there by boat to a deserted place by Himself. But when the multitudes heard it, they followed Him on foot from the cities. And when Jesus went out He saw a great multitude; and He was moved with compassion for them, and healed their sick. When it was evening, His disciples came to Him, saying, "This is a deserted place, and the hour is already late. Send the multitudes away, that they may go into the villages and buy themselves food." But Jesus said to them, "They do not need to go away. You give them something to eat." And they said to Him, "We have here only five loaves and two fish." He said, "Bring them here to Me." Then He commanded the multitudes to sit down on the grass. And He took the five loaves and the two fish, and looking up to heaven, He blessed and broke and gave the loaves to the disciples; and the disciples gave to the multitudes. So they all ate and were filled, and they took up twelve baskets full of the fragments that remained. Now those who had eaten were about five thousand men, besides women and children* (Matthew 14:13-21).

Matthew says that Jesus went to "a deserted place by Himself." Why? He had just been informed of the death of His cousin, John the Baptist. John had been beheaded at the order of Herod because of a rash and foolish promise Herod had made to his stepdaughter (see Mt. 14:1-12). Can you imagine the effect this had on Jesus? Being very human, Jesus certainly felt shock and grief at the news of John's brutal, senseless death.

The Scriptures tell us something very significant in the words "He departed to a deserted place by Himself." Jesus went out to be alone with His Father. He felt the need to get away by Himself—away from the crowds, the clamor, the sickness, the opposition—to pray and get the mind of His Father on this atrocity.

Jesus got alone to pray. There is a lesson here for every Christian. If you wish to be a powerful man or woman of God—a "breakout" person—there must be those times when you go to an isolated place to meet with God. Only as you shut out the clamoring voices of this world and seek the voice of your heavenly Father and His wisdom and plan for your circumstance or situation can you overcome an impossibility mind-set that says, "There's no hope; it can't be done."

I think back to the day when my father, at the age of 72, was dying. I had been called to the hospital because the doctor said that there was no hope my father would live. So I flew home and stopped at my parents' home before going to the hospital. While I was having a cup of tea with my mother, she received a call that my father had taken a turn for the worst and was hemorrhaging in the brain. When Mother got off the phone, I immediately took her hands and said, "Do you believe that if we pray, Jesus Christ will raise Dad up?"

My little Baptist mother looked into my eyes and said, "Yes, I believe." That's all Jesus needed to hear. So my mother and I knelt on the kitchen floor and I prayed a powerful prayer in the name of Jesus and we went off to the hospital.

When we arrived at the hospital, my father was dying—he was just taking his last breath. Following God's leading in my heart, I anointed my father with oil. (By this time my father was clinically dead.) Then I prayed in the name of Jesus because there is power in His name. After I finished praying, I instantly said to my mother, although it didn't look like my father was better except that he had started to breathe a little bit, "Now, we need to go home." "Yes," she said, "we need to go home." (By this time is was nighttime.)

As I walked out of the room, an unbelieving uncle who had been in the room with us came out after me and started to speak quite rudely to me. "You call yourself a minister of the gospel; you call yourself a man of God," he said, "yet you're leaving your father here to die." I said, "That's where you are wrong. I'm not leaving him here to die. I've prayed the prayer of faith and he's still alive. He's going to live." Then my mother and I walked out of the hospital, went home, went to bed, and slept all night—without receiving a call from the hospital telling us that my father had died.

The next morning we went to the hospital, and my father was much, much better. He smiled at us and said a few words to us. The next day I went back to my work. Later my mother sent me a photograph that she had taken of my father eight days after I had prayed for him in the hospital. In the picture he was wheeling a load of bricks down his garden path.

Until you learn God's perspective on your particular problem or need, you will always be overwhelmed with impossibilities and unable to handle life's situations. The best way to learn His perspective is to get away from all the clamor of society with its problems and impossible situations and enter your secret place with God so you can hear His voice.

God wants you to hear His voice. He has promised to guide you with His counsel (see Ps. 16:7; Is. 28:29). Too often, however, you may not hear His voice because you fail to "take time to be holy"—to run to your heavenly Father and pray to Him in secret. Instead, you try to battle your way through life's difficulties without knowing God's perspective on your needs. When you live this way, you most likely major in negative, impossible thinking. Jesus was, is, and always will be the greatest possibility thinker. There is much you can learn from how He handled the days following the death of John the Baptist.

Remember that Jesus had gone away to be alone with His Father. Still He wasn't able to escape the crowds for very long. They found Him, even in His deserted place. Note what happened when Jesus saw the multitude that had followed Him. The Scriptures say that He had compassion for them and healed their sick.

How long did this take? No one knows. It probably took quite a while, though, because Matthew says that the *men* in the crowd numbered 5,000. The passage doesn't say how many women and children were there, but Jesus could have faced a throng of 8,000, 10,000, or even more.

An impossibility thinker would have pushed the panic button when he saw the large crowd in front of him, and he might have responded in one of three ways: "Look at the size of that crowd! I'm only one person; what can I do?" or "I'm not going out to that crowd! I'm just not in the mood to be around other people right now," or "Send the people away! I can't have a healing meeting today—I need healing myself." Instead, Jesus looked beyond the reasons He couldn't meet the crowd and saw before Him the great possibilities for ministry. He found the reasons why He should do something. So laying aside His own grief and sorrow, He took compassion on the people and healed them.

Jesus' disciples, however, were another story. They were limited by their lack of imagination, the common problem of impossibility thinkers. The only things they could see were the negatives of the situation. Look at their statements:

- *This is a deserted place.* They had seen Jesus open blind eyes, unstop deaf ears, loosen dumb tongues, and do all sorts of other miracles. Now they saw no way to feed the multitude because there was no provision in the desert. They still did not understand that with Jesus there, every provision was available. Where God is present, it doesn't matter whether it is a desert or a fruitful field. The resources for provision are there.

- *The hour is already late.* What a ridiculous statement! God doesn't live in time; He lives in eternity. If you are His child, so do you. Time doesn't matter. You have whatever time God has allotted for your lifespan. It is important then that you buy up the time you have (see Eph. 5:16; Col. 4:5), using it wisely for the glory of God and making the most of every opportunity.
- *Send the multitudes away.* In the face of "impossible" circumstances, impossibility thinkers often opt to do nothing at all. To them that seems better than trying and failing.
- *Let them go into the villages and buy themselves food.* That sounds reasonable, doesn't it? The word *reasonable* means to be in accordance with reason; not excessive or extreme. To the impossibility mentality of the disciples, sending the people away to buy food was the only reasonable course of action.

Given their mind-set, the disciples no doubt were shocked when Jesus said to them, "They do not need to go away. You give them something to eat" (Mt. 14:16). Their amazement is reflected in their protest: "We have here only five loaves and two fish" (Mt. 14:17). Nevertheless, they brought the food to Jesus, who looked up toward Heaven, blessed the food, and broke it. The astounded disciples then served a meal to every person there and gathered 12 baskets full of the remains.

You may ask: How can I become a possibility thinker like Jesus? The answer lies in "looking up to heaven." That's the secret. Then you depend on the Lord and His power and resources instead of your own. As these Scriptures reveal, God's power and resources are considerable:

For with God nothing will be impossible (Luke 1:37)

I say to you, if you have faith as a mustard seed, you will say to this mountain, "Move from here to there," and it will move; and nothing will be impossible for you (Matthew 17:20b).

I can do all things through Christ who strengthens me....And my God shall supply all your need according to His riches in glory by Christ Jesus (Philippians 4:13,19).

"We've Never Done It That Way"

Another problem area that is similar to an impossibility mentality is narrow thinking. This attitude assumes that things must continue to be done in the same way time after time and year after year. A narrow-thinking person has limited imagination and creativity and allows very little latitude for change or disagreement. He is not necessarily hostile to change, but the thought that things could be any different simply never occurs to him. That's the curse of narrow thinking: The limited scope of an individual's thought processes prevents his mind from considering broader possibilities.

> Your expectations for the future are shaped by your experiences of the past.

Judging from my experience and contact with people all over the world, I believe that most western Christians are contained within themselves. If you are one of these many people, you are bound up by habits, thought patterns, and attitudes about yourself and others that limit your potential. Most of the time you probably are not even aware of these limiting characteristics. You are content simply to go along with the status quo. Therefore, you expect very little from God or your faith in the way of dynamic power or supernatural visitation, and your expectations for the future are shaped by your experiences of the past.

For example, you may be contained by narrow thinking regarding the miraculous in daily Christian life. You do not expect to see miracles because you have never witnessed or experienced one before and because your church has taught you that miracles ceased with the close of the New Testament era in the first century. If this is true for you, the concept that God could invade your life today with demonstrations of power and glory as in biblical days is completely foreign to you.

I remember the story of one young man who had broken out of containment in this area. When he visited our church in 1998, he testified that he had gone home one day and discovered that he had been robbed. First he started to laugh; then he reminded God of the promise, "If you ask anything in My name, I will do it" (Jn. 14:14); finally he prayed, "God, cause that fellow to bring that stuff all back again."

Now you know and I know that the worse thing a robber could ever think of is somebody discovering who he is; but the next day, the young man who had been robbed got a phone call. The guy on the phone said, "I don't know what's going on, but I had quite a night last night, and I've got to bring all that stuff back again." So the young man's belongings were restored to him! That's faith. That's believing that God's power can enter our lives today and make a difference.

Unfortunately, because many in the Church are narrow thinkers, they don't expect God to intervene miraculously in their lives. Or they expect Him to do the same thing every time because He did it that way once before. This may be why many Christians resist the genuine movement of God's Spirit in revival. They believe that the new revival movement cannot be God because it is different in scope, method, or appearance from a previous one.

If you are one of these contained Christians, today is the day to break out and give God room to do whatever, however, whenever He wants to do it. God is infinitely creative. Even the most cursory examination of the great variety in the created order demonstrates this. God delights in variety. He is always doing the unexpected and revealing that things are not always as they seem to human eyes. The prophet Isaiah wrote:

> *I am the Lord, your Holy One, the Creator of Israel, your King....Do not remember the former things, nor consider the things of old.* ***Behold, I will do a new thing,*** *now it shall spring forth; shall you not know it?* ***I will*** *even* ***make a road in the wilderness*** *and* ***rivers in the desert*** (Isaiah 43:15,18-19).

The Holy Spirit is a spirit of creativity and release, of life and freedom. Paul wrote, "Now the Lord is the Spirit; and where the Spirit of the Lord is, there is liberty" (2 Cor. 3:17). Satan, on the other hand, is a spirit of constraint, limitation, and bondage. He strives to prevent you from recognizing and exercising your full freedom in Christ and fulfilling your entire potential in Him.

From early in my ministry, I have resisted this bondage of narrow thinking. I have regularly sought to move beyond my limited experiences and ideas of who God is and how He operates so that I can embrace new potential and possibilities. I understand that God's redemptive purpose in the world never changes, but His ways and methods for accomplishing His purpose often do.

This breakout is evident in the church I pastor today. Even though I am in my 70's, I pastor a contemporary church that has attracted crowds of young people simply because I refuse to be contained by past concepts of what church life and structure ought to be.

For example, all over the western world, churches are trying to stir their people to bring the lost into the church to hear the gospel. In truth, the reverse sometimes needs to happen. We need to get the Body of Christ to go out into the community and become involved so that we can reach the lost and bring them to Christ where they are. This is what we have done in our church. We have reached out to people where they are, rather than expecting them to come to us. This has taken many forms.

Street teams spend one afternoon a week distributing the "Jesus" video, and there is a follow-up visit when the recipients have had time to review it. This has resulted in decisions for Christ. Other teams work the streets talking to people on a one-to-one basis–a most fruitful way of reaching people. Emphasis is on building relationships until people have confidence to share their lives. Visiting the blocks of apartments near our church has also resulted in good contact. It was during one of these visits that we discovered a community of Russian immigrants with a poor understanding of English who never went out anywhere because they were too afraid. Last Christmas we arranged a bus to pick these people up and brought them to the street party we organize for our local community.

Another of the major branches of the ministry is our City Care. As the name suggests, the aim of this ministry is to meet the needs of the less fortunate by supplying food and clothing. All forms of counseling by trained counselors are freely available and many of the community take advantage of this service.

In the early days of my ministry in New Zealand, it was common to think small. All the churches were small and the music concerts they sponsored were amateurish—and we rarely dreamed of anything different. Indeed, a church of 100 was considered to be large, and a church of 5,000—such as there was in those days in Stockholm, Sweden—was staggering to the imagination.

I no longer expect most churches to be small. God led me into this attitude change when I was still a pastor in New Zealand. It was two or three years after I had received the baptism of the Spirit, and I was pastoring a small church of 60 people. I was already on the track of doing radical things, so I went to my church board and told them that I wanted to hold a series of meetings in the city hall. At first they didn't think that we could do it, but I got them enthused and we proceeded to do some advertising and to organize a small, contemporary (for those days) choir.

On the first Sunday night, we filled the ground floor (that was hundreds of people compared to the 60 of our congregation) and many people were saved. By the last night people were seated in the balcony and many new members had been added to our church. Then I bought a large tent and set it up in various parts of the city over the summer months and added considerably more people to the Body of Christ. These were new ideas at the time, real "breakout" thinking. If I had remained locked into a narrow mode of thinking or expectation, none of this would have happened.

Today there is much more breakout than there used to be. We are seeing things around the world unlike anything the Church has seen since Pentecost. Great conventions and conferences draw thousands. Contemporary bands and high quality Christian music of all kinds abound. Churches everywhere are discovering the ways and means of breaking the barriers, of moving beyond the containment of their narrow thinking and expectations and daring to be different. This is good, but there is so much more yet to come.

"This Is Good Enough"

Much of western society today is characterized by a general decline of values and standards in every area of life, and many people no longer require or expect from themselves or others the high ethical and moral behavior of a generation ago. Mediocrity has become more and more accepted as the normal level of life and experience. Unfortunately, the modern Church has not been immune to this regression and has fallen prey to a third kind of mental containment: What we have, what we are doing, is good enough.

Sadly, many Church people take for granted the low, ordinary plane on which they live; they have no idea that they could be living on a much higher plane. God has much more for you than the mediocre level of the world. Consider what Paul said to the Christians at Ephesus:

> *But God, who is rich in mercy, because of His great love with which He loved us, even when we were dead in trespasses, made us alive together with Christ (by grace you have been saved), and raised us up together, and made us sit together in the heavenly places in Christ Jesus, that in the ages to come He might show the exceeding riches of His grace in His kindness toward us in Christ Jesus* (Ephesians 2:4-7).

Look what God has given you: mercy, love, life with Christ, a seat with Him in heavenly places, the "exceeding riches of His grace," and kindness. With all these blessings, why should you be content to think and live at the mediocre level of those who are not the sons and daughters of God? Yet that is precisely the level where many, if not most, Christians live. Due to the current and continuing great move of God's Spirit worldwide, things are beginning to change, but the change is slow and we still have a long way to go.

Many of the values and much of the mind-set of the world have filtered into the Church, sometimes so subtly that we are hardly aware of them. For example, we have become an incredibly entertainment-conscious age, and many believers spend much more time pursuing entertainment than they spend in the Word of God or in prayer. Hours in front of the television set have dulled the senses of many of us so that we do not think for ourselves anymore. All we want is to be entertained and to let the television people do our thinking for us. Now I don't think it's a sin to be entertained, but I do think it has the capacity to take from us that ability to touch Heaven the way that we should be touching it.

God wants to take you to a higher plane of living, which requires a higher plane of thinking. He has given you an amazing power to think and act creatively, something the average person rarely does. As man has educated himself more and more, he has lost much of his ability to sense God, thus becoming dependent upon himself rather than on God. You need to develop the capacities God has given you while maintaining your sense of dependence on Him. You do this by continually remembering and returning to God, who created you in His image and likeness and who wants you to use all He has given you for His glory.

The early Church was marked by a zeal and a passion to win the lost to Christ. One of the problems in many western world churches today is the lack of such passion. Many believers have become quite self-centered. In fact, mediocrity itself is, in a sense, a form of selfishness in that people seek gratification through the wrong types of pleasure and through other things that are not consistent with the Spirit of God. If you are focused on yourself, you cannot be focused on the lost. Nor will you stir yourself to change that condition.

A renewed passion for God must be stirred in you–and all members of the Body of Christ–before we can effectively reach out to bring in the lost. Unfortunately many churches try to stir their people to bring in the lost before the church members themselves are passionately seeking God. Only as the fires of revival are stoked in our lives will we be lifted to a higher plane of Christian experience and living. Then we will find greater fruitfulness as we go out to the lost in our communities.

Don't accept the mediocrity of the world. Break out into the higher plane of thinking and living that is the gift of God and your legacy as a believer. Don't settle for less than the best. Determine through the Spirit to become all that you can be in Christ.

Compartmentalized Thinking

Compartmentalized thinking, in which certain words and actions are appropriate for Sunday and others are used throughout the rest of the week, is also a type of mental containment. Usually this occurs because the people who come to church on Sunday are constrained by all kinds of bondages, many of which are rooted in fear and tradition (which we will talk about further in later chapters.)

For example, many Christians believe that dancing, clapping, and shouting are not appropriate in church–at least not on a Sunday morning in the sanctuary. These may be fine for a youth convention or an outdoor worship event, but most certainly not within the Sunday morning service. In fact, after one worship service I greeted a stranger who likened our worship to a circus and said that she would never come back because what she had witnessed was certainly not church. That fine lady is now a member of our church. God rescued her from compartmentalized thinking.

God has done the same for many people through what has come to be known as the Toronto blessing. Joy and laughter are becoming part of worship, and things that were previously relegated to the ridiculous—such as rolling on the floor like a barrel—are being accepted as evidence of the presence and blessing of God. This has done our church a world of good—and I don't think that we are alone. Lives are being changed as "religion" and "religious" are being redefined. People are being set free from thoughts and definitions concerning the Church and its life.

Perhaps it's time that you too redefine your expectations of worship. Don't be too quick to limit what God can do—and indeed, wants to do—on a Sunday morning. You just might be surprised when He meets you in an unexpected way and you find that your definitions of *sacred* and *profane* are changed forever.

"It's the Same Old Thing"

Boredom is a fifth form of mental containment. I never cease to be amazed by the number of Christians I meet or hear of who complain of boredom. They are bored at church, bored at home, bored at work, bored with life. Boredom affects every age group: children, young people, and adults. What seems even more surprising is that boredom is so prevalent in a time when more outlets exist than ever before for entertainment, recreation, social activities, and other opportunities.

Boredom is never from God. It isn't a strength or a blessing. To the contrary, boredom is bondage. God made us to laugh, enjoy, create, and think. He designed life so that it would be full of exciting things every day.

> **Many people in the world, as busy and involved as they may be, are bored because they have devoted their lives to things that ultimately lack meaning and purpose.**

If you are a bored Christian, it's time for you to spend some prayerful moments evaluating your life. Why are you bored? Most likely the answer is that you are not using your God-given gifts to their fullest capacity.

Can you imagine the apostles Peter or Paul saying that they were bored? Certainly not! Their lives were too full of God's activity to be boring. Please notice that I said "God's activity" not just "activity." Being busy and active is not enough because activities in and of themselves can never adequately satisfy you. The pursuit of the things of the world for their own sake never brings lasting contentment. Life has no meaning outside of Christ; no purpose apart from God. Therefore, many people in the world, as busy and involved as they may be, are bored because they have devoted their lives to things that ultimately lack meaning and purpose.

So there really is no reason for you ever to be bored. God is never bored, and He created you in His image. There is so much to do, so much to learn, so many challenges to face, so many opportunities to pursue that there is no time to be bored. Besides, God did not create you for boredom, but for abundance. Jesus said, "I have come that they may have life, and that they may have it more abundantly" (Jn. 10:10b). By "they" Jesus refers to His "sheep," His followers for whom He is the "door" and the "good Shepherd." How can a person be bored if he has an abundance of life? That's life to its fullest, life with everything that God intended it should be.

Why then, you may be asking, am I bored? I believe there are several reasons. First, bored Christians have lost sight of who they really are in Christ. Paul reminds us that as Christians we are "children of God, and if children, then heirs; heirs of God and joint heirs with Christ" (Rom. 8:16b-17a). If you forget that you are God's child, you won't think like Him, talk like Him, or act like Him. Then the glorious life of the redeemed loses much of its luster and you become bored.

Another reason many Christians are bored is because they have grown too close to the things of this world. Once you have come to Christ, nothing else can satisfy you. Yet you may get caught up in pursuing worldly things with the same vigor that lost people do and find that you are soon thinking like the world. Then boredom sets in because nothing in the world can match the thrill and excitement of life you have known in the Spirit. This is why John cautions believers in his first letter:

> *Do not love the world or the things in the world. If anyone loves the world, the love of the Father is not in him. For all that is in the world; the lust of the flesh, the lust of the eyes, and the pride of life; is not of the Father but is of the world. And the world is passing away, and the lust of it; but he who does the will of God abides forever* (1 John 2:15-17).

A third reason Christians get bored is because they don't walk in the Spirit and get to know the Lord and His Word. Knowledge is a wonderful thing, and spiritual knowledge is the best kind of all. As you walk with God you learn to enjoy intimacy and fellowship with Him, as John testified, "That which we have seen and heard we declare to you, that you also may have fellowship with us; and truly our fellowship is with the Father and with His Son Jesus Christ" (1 Jn. 1:3). Then His life and Spirit fill your life and His Word fills your heart, and you are not bored because every day with Jesus is a new adventure.

I say all this to state that if you are bored, you are probably not living to your full capacity in God. If this is true, the following suggestions will help you to move beyond your boredom. First, remind yourself who you are in Christ and rekindle your passion for intimacy with Him. Second, remember your high and holy calling, the individual life mission that God has given you. Go over it in your thinking and in your prayers. Then look at your priorities and observe how the world has infringed on your faithfulness to fulfill the call God has placed on your life. Third, reaffirm the goals and vision God has given you. Be specific how you will do what God has called you to do, and if need be, readjust your goals or your schedule for reaching them.[1]

Finally, try this surefire way to beat boredom. Take your Bible and begin reading in Matthew's Gospel. When you have read all of Matthew, go to Mark, then Luke, then John. After the Gospels, read the Book of Acts. If you are serious, I guarantee that before you have finished reading Acts you won't be bored anymore. In fact, it will probably happen much sooner than that...maybe even before you complete Matthew. The Spirit will open your heart and mind to the infinite possibilities, opportunities, and challenges available to you–enough to fill ten lifetimes–and boredom will become a thing of the past. Try it for yourself and see if it isn't so.

No Christian who seriously and thoughtfully reads the Scriptures can possibly be bored because Christ has issued an inescapable challenge to live for others in His name. If we take God's Word seriously, we cannot live to ourselves. Our hearts will hunger and thirst not only for His righteousness but also to impart what we have read to a lost and dying world.

1. Lori Wilke, *Requirements for Greatness* (Shippensburg, PA: Destiny Image Publishers, 1996).

Break out from the mental chains of containment that bind you. Don't let an impossibility mentality, narrow thinking, mediocrity, compartmentalized thinking, or boredom rob you of your legacy in Christ. God has so much more for you than what you now have, know, or are. Let the mind of Christ transform and renew your mind and raise you to a new and higher plane–and begin today. Don't wait for some event or experience to force the issue!

Chapter 4

Removing Moses' Veil

In 1993 a medical specialist told me that I was going to go permanently blind very soon. My initial reaction to the news was one of horror. Images flashed through my mind of how terrible it would be to wake up every morning and not be able to see my wife, my children, or my grandchildren. There would be no more sunsets with their brilliant reds, oranges, and yellows; no more cloudless nights with moonlight reflecting off the sea. I would lose a great deal of my independence. My entire life would change in ways I hated to think about. Now it is certainly true that many, many blind people do remarkably well, learning to compensate with their other senses for the loss of their sight, but it still seemed to me that it would be a terrible thing to go physically blind.

After the initial shock and fear wore off, my faith and spiritual resources took over. In faith I made my stand against the doctor's prognosis and said, "It will not happen to me." I wasn't denying reality; rather, I refused to surrender to it. Instead, I claimed healing in Jesus' name. I also remembered a prophecy that had been spoken over me several months before, that I would be in the forefront of the next great outpouring of the Spirit of God. Throughout my convalescence, I kept reminding God and myself of that word.

God was faithful and fulfilled His promises. Over five years later, I still have my vision and I still have my health; and my church and I are enthusiastic participants in a Spirit-led renewal that is rapidly reaching global proportions.

There is something worse than physical blindness, though—spiritual blindness. Blindness of the eyes afflicts the physical body but is rarely directly life-threatening. Spiritual blindness, on the other hand, strikes at the very heart of man's nature and his relationship with God and negatively affects every other area of life. If left unchanged, it will end in eternal spiritual death. Spiritual blindness lies at the core of all sinful thoughts, motivations, and actions of mankind and is characteristic of the sinful nature we all share. Paul wrote to the Ephesians,

> *This I say, therefore, and testify in the Lord, that you should no longer walk as the rest of the Gentiles walk, in the futility of their mind, having their understanding darkened, being alienated from the life of God, because of the ignorance that is in them, because of the blindness of their heart; who, being past feeling, have given themselves over to lewdness, to work all uncleanness with greediness* (Ephesians 4:17-19).

Truly it is an awful thing to be spiritually blind. Paul describes the lost as walking "in the futility of their mind, having their understanding darkened," ignorant of spiritual truth "because of the blindness of their heart." Spiritual blindness is the inability to understand spiritual truth and reality. Paul told the Corinthian church that unsaved people do not accept the gospel because they lack the spiritual discernment necessary to understand it (see 1 Cor. 2:14). Without spiritual vision, intellectual knowledge is all there is, and that counts very little. True vision comes only as the Holy Spirit brings illumination to the heart.

> Intellectual knowledge counts for very little in the absence of spiritual vision.

The Veiled Gospel

The apostle Paul certainly understood the contrast between spiritual light and spiritual darkness. In his second letter to Corinth he wrote,

> *Therefore, since we have this ministry, as we have received mercy, we do not lose heart. But we have renounced the hidden things of*

shame, not walking in craftiness nor handling the word of God deceitfully, but by manifestation of the truth commending ourselves to every man's conscience in the sight of God. But even if our gospel is veiled, it is veiled to those who are perishing, whose minds the god of this age has blinded, who do not believe, lest the light of the gospel of the glory of Christ, who is the image of God, should shine on them (2 Corinthians 4:1-4).

Paul knew what he was talking about because he himself had experienced blindness and been set free. As Saul of Tarsus and a proud Pharisee he had relentlessly pursued and persecuted Christians, believing in blind zeal that he was serving God. While on his way to Damascus on just such a mission, he was struck down on the road by the powerful presence of the risen Christ. His encounter with the Lord left him physically blind.

Saul endured three days of physical blindness as he fasted and prayed and as the Spirit enlightened him to the truths concerning Jesus. Finally a believer named Ananias came to Saul, laid hands on him, and prayed for him, and Saul regained his sight. Now the Pharisee saw things in a completely new light. He received spiritual light in his soul. So dramatic and thorough was the change that Saul the Pharisee became Paul the apostle and evangelist. (Read Acts 9:1-22.)

The point is that Paul received light in his spirit, light in his soul. Having received this light, he understood that the gospel is "veiled to those who are perishing" (2 Cor. 4:3), meaning that the gospel message is concealed from the understanding of the lost. Why? It is not by God's desire but because satan, the "god of this age," has blinded their minds.

This veil of spiritual blindness is the reason why a believer may witness to someone, and he or she can't seem to understand what is being said. For example, the unbeliever may give the witness a blank stare, ask irrelevant questions, or try to change the subject. Perhaps you have had this experience. If you have, you probably discovered that some people just are not interested in hearing the gospel, and others are downright hostile. This happens because the person with whom you are speaking is spiritually blind. Anyone who accepts Christ does so because the Holy Spirit removes the "veil" from his heart, making faith and spiritual understanding possible. It is the Holy Spirit who draws people to Jesus; no one comes to Him apart from the Spirit's work (see 2 Cor. 3:16).

Therefore, a firm conviction has grown in me over the years that it is not very effective simply to witness to one person after another in a hit-or-miss fashion. Everyone *needs* to hear the gospel, but not everyone is *ready* to hear. Certainly you need to plant seeds in hearts by sharing Christ as you have opportunity. Your witness will be more effective, however, if you regularly pray, "God, lead me to people who are ready to hear and ready to accept the good news of Jesus." Then you will find that He places a burden on your heart for a particular person or causes that person to cross your path.

I once heard a story that confirms this truth. A man stood in the street and asked the Lord to show him who among the people passing by were Christians and who were not. As God revealed one believer after another, the man approached each person and asked, "Do you believe in Jesus?" Of the dozen or so people whom he approached, each one replied that he or she was a believer. Not once was he wrong.

If God can do that, can He not surely do the same to show you unbelievers who are ready, or almost ready, to receive the Lord Jesus? I believe that He can, and that He will prepare the hearts of those to whom He leads you.

I must caution you, however, that not everyone to whom God leads you to share the gospel will accept the Lord Jesus in his heart. Jesus made this clear in His parable of the sower (see Mt. 13:3-9,18-23). As tragic as this is, it is a fact you must accept. No matter how much you wish it were otherwise, not every person on the earth is going to accept Jesus Christ as Savior. Multitudes will go to hell.

God in His perfect foreknowledge knows who these people are. Since He is omniscient–knowing all things past, present, and future–He sees who will accept Him and who will reject Him. Yet He is "not willing that any should perish but that all should come to repentance" (2 Pet. 3:9b). That's God's passion. That's His heart. So in mercy, He extends opportunity to all people to be saved from the clutches of satan.

Your task is to be a true and faithful witness to the Lord Jesus Christ. The world will not hear of Him unless you and I tell them. Unfortunately, many Christians have poor track records for faithfulness in witnessing to the world. Often this happens because they are spiritually blind.

Spiritual Blindness in the Church

Have you ever considered that you are spiritually blind? Spiritual blindness is nothing more or less than a form of containment.

Even after you have become a Christian through trusting Christ as your Savior, and even after you have been Spirit-baptized and Spirit-filled, you can still be a victim of spiritual blindness in some area of your life.

Satan knows that he can do nothing to take away your salvation, but he works quite hard to keep you from moving into full maturity in Christ. If he can keep you in the dark regarding some spiritual truth, he will. Your area of blindness is most likely different from mine, nevertheless we are both impeded in our spiritual walk of faith. Satan causes this blindness in several ways. First, the circumstances and events you experience can either impede or aid your growth in the Lord, depending upon how you respond in any given situation. Sickness, the loss of loved ones, the loss of a job, and raising a physically or emotionally handicapped child are but a few of these emotionally difficult situations that may influence spiritual growth.

A second factor is the depth and quality of the biblical preaching and teaching you have received. Consistent, high-quality focus on the Bible promotes mature disciples.

A third factor that affects your level of spiritual maturity—which is probably the most significant influence—is the choices you have made regarding such things as Bible study, prayer, worship, and obedience to the voice of God's Spirit within you.

Biblical Ignorance

Ignorance of God's Word is a serious source of spiritual blindness for many Christians. I remember one meeting in a fairly small church where I asked one person after another how often they read the Bible. I was amazed. One person said, "I don't read it very much," and another said, "Well, I read the Bible now and then." Still others said that they read the Bible once a week or maybe twice a week. Just two or three people said that they read the Word of God every day. This was a fairly stable church with a good pastor and a growing attendance. The members were fervent in worship, with great praising and shouting. Yet, they didn't read the Bible. Talk about containment. Satan was containing those dear folks by their failure to read the Scriptures.

How about you? How important is the Bible to you? What place does it have in your life? Do you read it spasmodically every now and then with no pattern to your reading, or do you try to spend some time in it every day in a systematic way?

Your answers to these questions will reveal much about the degree to which you walk in victory or defeat each day because knowing, understanding, and applying God's Word is essential to victorious Christian living. When Jesus was in the wilderness being tempted by the devil, He was in the power of the Spirit. Yet He still used Scripture to answer and defeat satan's temptations.

The psalmist also learned the importance of using the Scriptures to resist the evil one, for he said, "Your word I have hidden in my heart, that I might not sin against You" (Ps. 119:11), and "Your word is a lamp to my feet and a light to my path" (Ps. 119:105). He relied on the truth of God's Word to lead Him "in the paths of righteousness" (Ps. 23:3) and away from the ways of a wicked man, who "in his proud countenance does not seek God; God is in none of his thoughts" (Ps. 10:4).

If you find yourself prone to give in to persistent temptations; if you have trouble remembering Scripture verses when you need them to face tough situations; if you sometimes feel as though you are stumbling around in the dark not knowing which way to turn or where to go, you are very likely suffering from spiritual blindness where God's Word is concerned. The truth of His Word is not penetrating your heart because satan has contained you.

This containment may be as simple as an overextended schedule that prevents you from making the study of the Scriptures a daily priority. Or the constraints the enemy has imposed on you may permit you to read the Word but with a lack of understanding. Or yet again, you may suffer from hardness of heart in some area or be bound by some iniquity that prevents you from receiving and obeying the Word of truth as you read. In each case satan has blinded you to the truth of your condition. Once you see how you have been contained, you must make a decision whether or not you are going to permit satan to continue his deception.

If a busy schedule is your problem, ruthlessly evaluate each part of your day. What can you eliminate or rearrange to give you a block of uninterrupted time to study God's Word? If at first you don't see anything you can change, ask God to help you see your schedule through His eyes. Then make the changes as He leads. If you are sincere, the Holy Spirit will reveal the truth to you and show you what changes you must make. Yes, the pathway of change may be hard at first, but persevere and you will see the rewards of making the study of God's Word a priority in your life.

If you regularly read God's Word but lack understanding, carefully evaluate how you study God's Word. Do you make it your practice to pray before you read, asking the Lord to speak to you through His Word? He has promised that the Holy Spirit who lives within you "will guide you into all truth" (John 16:13), so you have a Helper who is always ready to reveal the truth contained in the Bible. Or perhaps you have difficulty understanding the Bible because you don't know what all the words mean. If this is the case, it's time that you get a good Bible dictionary or that you read difficult verses in more than one version. Using a Bible with a good system of cross references can also be helpful because then you can find other verses that pertain to the same topic.

Finally, make it your practice every day to pray as David did: "Search me, O God, and know my heart; try me, and know my anxieties; and see if there is any wicked way in me, and lead me in the way everlasting" (Ps. 139:23-24). Such a prayer, offered in sincerity, will surely cure the third type of containment–the presence of sin and iniquity in your heart–that satan may be using to keep you from receiving and obeying the Word of God.

You do not have to live in spiritual blindness. The abundant life and health that God has designed you for may be as close as your decision to make a commitment to spend time every day reading God's Word, to seek the guidance of the Holy Spirit as you read, to use whatever helps you understand what you read, and to allow the Spirit of God to search your heart for any sin that might prevent the seed of truth from being rooted and watered in your heart. Then, as the Word of truth begins to find room in your heart, remind yourself throughout the day of what you learned in your reading and look for opportunities to apply it in your life. Breakout from spiritual containment due to biblical ignorance will soon follow.

Prayerlessness

Prayerlessness is an even greater cause of spiritual containment for Christians than ignorance of God's Word. You may wonder why this is so. I believe that a lack of faith is often at the root of prayerlessness. Too many Christians don't really expect God to answer, or they assume that a need is too small for God to be concerned with.

This is tragic because there is no reason for these attitudes. The Scriptures abundantly reveal both the power of prayer and the certainty that God is concerned about all aspects of our lives. Consider, for example, these words of Jesus:

> *Again I say to you that if two of you agree on earth concerning anything that they ask, it will be done for them by My Father in heaven* (Matthew 18:19).
>
> *If you ask anything in My name, I will do it* (John 14:14)
>
> *Now if God so clothes the grass of the field, which today is, and tomorrow is thrown into the oven, will He not much more clothe you, O you of little faith? Therefore do not worry, saying, "What shall we eat?" or "What shall we drink?" or "What shall we wear?" For after all these things the Gentiles seek. For your heavenly Father knows that you need all these things. But seek first the kingdom of God and His righteousness, and all these things shall be added to you* (Matthew 6:30-32).

Please note the words *anything* and *all things* in these verses. God's promise to hear and answer our prayers and to meet the needs of our lives applies not just to *some*things, but to *all* things. This attitude of bringing everything to God in prayer was certainly evident in Jesus' earthly ministry. Time and again the Gospels tell us that Jesus withdrew to pray (see Mt. 14:23; Mk 1:35; 6:46; Lk. 5:16; 6:12; 9:18,28; 11:1). In all things, large and small, He sought the guidance and strength of His Father.

Do you have such a relationship with the Lord Jesus that you not only know His Word but believe that He will be faithful to accomplish it in your life? Is prayer your first response when you are faced with a difficulty or is it your last? Your honest answers to these questions can reveal quite clearly both the depth of your relationship with the Lord Jesus Christ and your attitude concerning prayer. Indeed, they are a pretty good gauge of your spiritual maturity as a whole because prayer is essential in your relationship with God.

Perhaps you know today that you have been contained by the enemy of your soul into prayerlessness. You seldom pray, and when you do, you do all the talking concerning things that relate solely to you. Tell God that you want to be faithful in prayer, if indeed this is the desire of your heart. Ask Him to give you opportunities to pray that strengthen your faith in both His willingness and His ability to answer your prayers. Then respond when He lays people and situations on your heart that you would not previously have thought to pray for. You will be overwhelmed both by the mercy and love that

God shows to you and by the mercy and love that He begins to build in your own heart as He takes you beyond the things and people you used to pray for.

Over the past few years, God has been doing this in me. He has been taking me out of the container in which I had boxed myself (and Him) and has been causing me to pray about people and things that I had never prayed for. For example, He put on my heart the alcoholics I see every morning as I pass through a certain part of town on my way to the church. There are so many of them, some who are very young and others who are quite old. Most of them look quite decrepit and ill. By the grace of God I have been praying for them every day. And should the Lord tell me to go among them and share the love of Jesus with them, I know that I'll do it because God has been working in my heart while I've been praying for these alcholics. He's been building spiritual maturity in me.

God will do the same for you if you'll let Him. He'll show you the incredible power of prayer by giving you someone or something to pray for, and then changing you as you pray. One day you'll discover that you truly have broken out of spiritual containment because you will find yourself praying for the co-worker who falsely accuses you of stealing and tries to get you fired, for the young man who breaks into your car and steals your packages, or for the alcoholic who rams into your car while he is drunk. Prayer will have become the lifeline that God originally intended it to be in your life, and you'll find yourself taking everything and anything to God in prayer and believing that He will hear and meet your need—even if the answer is a long time in coming. You'll also discover that the days of praying because it is a required duty or an expected ritual will be but a memory because you will have experienced the guidance and wisdom that cannot come apart from the Holy Spirit within you. Then, when you are met by a need for which there are no words or a situation that persists despite countless prayers, you will not resort to prayerlessness, the response of the many who find it far easier to pray nothing than to earnestly seek the wisdom of God and persist until the answer comes.

Countless times I have experienced the power of such prayer guided or spoken by the Spirit of God Himself. One such time was when I was doing a crusade in Hamilton, New Zealand, where the power of God wrought such a major breakthrough that on nearly every street of the city lived someone who had been saved, healed, or filled with the Holy Spirit.

Yet, in the middle of that crusade, one particular woman seemed to remain untouched by God's saving, healing, delivering power. This woman, a woman with a spirit of infirmity much like the woman spoken of in Luke's Gospel (see Lk. 13:11-13), hopped onto the platform and sought prayer one night early in the crusade. So I sat her in a chair and prayed for her and prayed for her and prayed for her...and nothing happened. The next night she was back, and I prayed for her again...and nothing happened. When she came up for prayer the third night, I prayed in my heart, "Lord Jesus, there is a reason why this woman is not getting healed." Then the Holy Spirit said to me, "She is in bondage to sin." So I said to the lady, "Ma'am, have you given your life to Jesus Christ and confessed your sin to Him?" She said, "No, I never have." So I said to her, "Before I shout at the devil that is binding you, will you give your life to Jesus Christ?" She said yes and prayed a sinner's prayer from her heart. Then I laid my hand on her head and said, "In the mighty name of Jesus, you spirit of palsy, come out of her." And the power of God threw her off the chair and onto the floor, right unto her back. Because of the severe curve in her back, she rocked back and forth, each time with her back becoming straighter until her feet and her head were on the floor at the same time. Then she leaped to her feet and was totally healed by the power of God.

Now, what if that woman had lost faith after the first night and had not returned? Or what if I had not sought the wisdom of the Holy Spirit to know what to pray for her on that third night? That precious woman would not have been healed during that crusade.

Faith in the release of the wisdom and power of God through prayer brought healing into that woman's life. The same thing can happen for you. The Scriptures promise that "those who seek the Lord shall not lack any good thing" (Ps. 34:10b.) That includes you and your need–even if it's a need that you see no answer for or you've prayed about time and again. Don't give up because the answer is longer in coming that you would like. Rather, make the choice to cling to the Word of God, which promises:

> *Ask, and it will be given to you; seek, and you will find; knock, and it will be opened to you. For everyone who asks receives,*

> *and he who seeks finds, and to him who knocks it will be opened* (Matthew 7:7-8).
>
> *Likewise the Spirit also helps in our weaknesses. For we do not know what we should pray for as we ought, but the Spirit Himself makes intercession for us with groanings which cannot be uttered* (Romans 8:26).
>
> *If any of you lacks wisdom, let him ask of God, who gives to all liberally and without reproach, and it will be given to him. But let him ask in faith, with no doubting, for he who doubts is like a wave of the sea driven and tossed by the wind* (James 1:5-6).

Satan would like to use such opportunities to sow discouragement into your life so that you are blinded to the importance, the power, and the effectiveness of prayer and are contained through prayerlessness. Don't let him! Break out with a renewed commitment to exercise the privilege and the gifts that are yours through prayer.

Dead Worship

A third area where spiritual containment is often revealed is in worship. Dead, dry "worship" dulls the spiritual sight and sensitivity of Christians. This is "worship" where God is contained by a prescribed ritual or schedule. Revitalized worship, on the other hand, gives evidence of God's presence in the midst of His people and brings with it a greater awareness of the power of God and the wideness of His mercy and love toward His children.

In recent years, and particularly during the current move of God, churches and Christians all over the world have begun to rediscover the wonder of God-directed worship. When God is free to meet His people when and how He chooses, exciting, amazing, surprising things begin to happen and worship becomes far more than an hour on Sunday morning that is filled in a predicatable manner.

King David, one of the most lavish worshipers of all times, said, "I was glad when they said to me, 'Let us go into the house of the Lord' " (Ps. 122:1). David obviously found great joy in worshiping God. Is the same true for you? Is worship an exciting time for you? Do you look forward to it and enter in joyfully, singing and praising the Lord from your heart? Do you expect God to meet you as you worship and do you give Him permission to do whatever He wants to do? Is your heart touched by His presence and your love for Him poured out liberally, with little or no concern for what others might think of you?

If not, your worship is contained because God's Spirit within you is contained. So closely have you regimented everything that happens when you and God meet that God has little or no room to show you His love, mercy, and power. Indeed, He may not be able to reveal His presence at all, so tightly have you boxed Him in.

Today is the day to ask God to reveal Himself to you in a new and different way. You might want to start by doing something out of the ordinary as you worship Him, such as lifting your hands, dancing, or kneeling before Him. Then let God take over and meet you as He will.

Flesh or Spirit?

Finally, the degree to which satan has contained you spiritually will be visible in the choices you make every day. Each time you choose to listen to the voice of the Holy Spirit within you instead of the voice of your old sinful nature, you move a step closer to spiritual maturity.

This struggle to obey God is an ongoing battle that will continue throughout life. Whenever you start to walk in obedience to the Spirit in some new area of life and deliberately work to break out of your containment, you will face a mighty struggle inside. This happens because the new nature you received when you were saved, the nature of the Spirit, resists your old sinful nature, the nature of the flesh. Without a doubt, the new Spirit-nature is the stronger, but which of the two prevails depends on the choices you make. If you continue to listen to and act on the call of the flesh, you will experience little growth and little victory, and your spiritual vision will be clouded and distorted. If, on the other hand, you listen to the Spirit and allow Him to work in your life, you will grow in your Christian life and experience the peace, power, and confidence that come from walking by the Spirit of God.

Paul likened this change within to the changing of clothes: "...put off...the old man which grows corrupt according to the deceitful lusts...and...put on the new man which was created according to God, in true righteousness and holiness" (Eph. 4:22,24). Thus, the power to walk in obedience is within your reach because the Lord has given you everything you need to walk in holiness; but the choice is yours. You must determine how serious you are about breaking free from the spiritual blindness and containment in which satan has bound you.

A couple from my church faced this decision the first time they came to our services. They were coming out of the church when, guided by the Spirit of God, I grabbed the young man just as he passed me and swung him around toward me. He was a bit startled as I said, "Good morning," but he said, "Good morning," as did the girl who was with him. Then I asked them, "Have you been here before?" "No," they replied, "we've never been here." Then out of my mouth popped these words, "How come you two are sleeping together?"

The young man's face went quite white and the girl's eyes filled with tears. Then the young man said, "Who told you that?" I said, "God." Then I spoke kindly to them, saying, "Look, I'm not pointing the finger. I'm not condemning you. Would you like to make an appointment to come see me?"

They made an appointment and came to my office the following week. As we talked that day, the girl said with tears in her eyes, "I hate doing what we've been doing. I come from a Pentecostal home, but I ran away from my parents and I wanted to run away from God and from church. But I have been doing something that I hate doing, and I want to make sure that I can get back to God." The young man then said to his girlfriend, "I'll not sleep with you again until we are married."

I discovered as we talked that the young man was not saved. I led him to the Lord in my office and also prayed with the young woman as she recommited her life to Jesus Christ. Later I conducted their wedding, and when the time came I dedicated two of their children. Praise God!

No one in my church, not even my wife, knows who these two people are. I've never told a living soul. I tell their story here simply to illustrate the kinds of decisions that each of us face every day, decisions that determine our spiritual destiny and maturity. Those two young people could have denied their sexual relationship. Or they could have pretended that they were married. Then what would I have done? I would have looked pretty stupid. Instead they chose to honestly face their sin and make a change.

This is the only choice that brings freedom from the spiritual blindness and containment that satan uses to keep us from going on in our walk with God. The young woman knew God. She knew that what she was doing was wrong. Yet, until that moment, she did not make the choice to obey God instead of her flesh.

It is only when we confess our sin and take the step of obedience that we can be freed from the bondage that satan has kept us in. You know your secret sins. Determine within your heart today to pursue holiness. Say, "God, help me live a holy life. I refuse to live locked in behind satan's wall of containment any longer." Then go for it with everything you've got, clinging tightly to the hand of Jesus all the way. He will do His best for you. He *will* set you free.

Breakout From Tradition and Legalism

Spiritual containment also comes through the traps of tradition and legalism, which are related. Tradition is an established or customary way of behavior, particularly as a religious practice, whereas legalism means strict or excessive conformity to a religious law or code. Jesus confronted both of these in His run-ins with the scribes and Pharisees.

Tradition is not necessarily bad. Often tradition is important to help us remember our purpose and keep our focus on who we are and where we have come from. It becomes a problem, however, when it loses meaning and is maintained as an end in itself. Then it is a hindrance to effective ministry. This is especially true when the tradition has no clear biblical mandate to begin with. For example, the observance of communion is a good tradition: It was clearly commanded by our Lord in the Scriptures and is an important reminder to us of what Jesus did for us on the cross and of our position as redeemed sinners. A problem tradition, on the other hand, might be an inflexible approach to worship: always doing it the same way, in the same order, in a very predictable manner.

Problems with tradition are found not only in "formal" churches, but also in Pentecostal, Charismatic, and non-Pentecostal evangelical churches. Any prescribed manner of behavior that restrains the work of the Holy Spirit during worship, preaching, or ministry times is a tradition that needs to be examined and changed. For example, one church I spoke at some years ago required the speaker to stay behind the pulpit and not walk around on the platform while he was speaking. Now, I like to move around as I speak. So this was a tradition that was limiting for me.

There are many other examples I could cite, but the point is this: A healthy congregation will periodically examine its traditions to see if anything needs to be changed. Unhealthy traditions dampen the work of the Holy Spirit. If a tradition not prescribed in the Scriptures has lost its meaning or purpose, get rid of it! If it is a tradition proscribed in the Bible but it has become cold or ritualistic, look for ways to revitalize it, restoring fire and meaning to its observance.

Legalism, unlike tradition, is never healthy. A legalistic mind-set has no room for compassion or mercy, only judgment. There is no "wiggle room." Such righteousness is measured by strict adherence to the rules and regulations, whether or not they are biblically based. Sometimes legalism develops from a zealous loyalty to tradition; other times from well-intentioned but misguided attempts to translate religious law into appropriate behavior.

Jesus reserved His harshest criticisms for legalistic observance of the law and for the religious leaders who practiced it. It was not that Jesus was opposed to the law; far from it. What He objected to was elevating love of the law to a higher place than love for God and for other people. Jesus said of Himself, "Do not think that I came to destroy the Law or the Prophets. I did not come to destroy but to fulfill" (Mt. 5:17). Jesus told His disciples,

> *The scribes and the Pharisees sit in Moses' seat. Therefore whatever they tell you to observe, that observe and do, but do not do according to their works; for they say, and do not do. For they bind heavy burdens, hard to bear, and lay them on men's shoulders; but they themselves will not move them with one of their fingers* (Matthew 23:2-4).

He pulled no punches with the religious leaders:

> *Woe to you, scribes and Pharisees, hypocrites! For you pay tithe of mint and anise and cummin, and have neglected the weightier matters of the law: justice and mercy and faith. These you ought to have done, without leaving the others undone* (Matthew 23:23).

The problem in Jesus' day was that over the years a multitude of little rules and regulations had been developed to surround the law and regulate people's behavior and actions. Intended to protect the law, these had become a burdensome weight on the people that actually hindered them from understanding and knowing God and His love.

The modern Church has not been immune to this problem. In my earlier years of ministry in New Zealand, when my wife and I were raising our five children, there were many activities that were considered a sin to do on Sundays. For example, it was a "sin" to go swimming on Sunday or to ride a streetcar or a bus because it forced the driver to work on Sunday. This was legalism. There was no biblical mandate concerning these things. They were examples of human attempts to interpret what was meant by the commandment, "Remember the Sabbath day, to keep it holy" (Ex. 20:8).

I remember hot summer Sundays when we would be in church all morning and afterward the other kids in the neighborhood would all go swimming. Our children couldn't, though, because they were the pastor's children and it was a "sin" to swim on a Sunday. One hot Sunday we were on our way home from church when I suddenly realized how stupid it was that other children could enjoy a cool swim and mine couldn't simply because it was Sunday. So I said to my wife, "We're going to break something here. Let's pack up a picnic basket and go to the river and let the kids have a swim." We had a great time. That night we had a wonderful service at church with people being saved and the blessings of God in evidence. We felt quite certain that God did not object to our Sunday swim.

Such areas of legalism abound. Many, if not all, church people are regularly contained by some religious idea or thought that is not backed up by Scripture. So take time to examine your attitudes and practices to see, first of all, if they are scriptural, and second, if they help or hinder people in coming to know the Lord. Breakout churches major on mercy, compassion, grace, and love rather than on rules; on the *spirit* rather than the *letter* of the law. Breakout churches are solidly biblical but understand with Paul that "love is the fulfillment of the law" (Rom. 13:10b).

Spiritual Visionaries

It is truly tragic when God's people stumble along in spiritual ignorance and blindness because it is so unnecessary. We have in us Christ Himself of whom John wrote, "In Him was life, and the life was the light of men. And the light shines in the darkness, and the darkness did not comprehend it" (Jn. 1:4-5). The "light of men" shines in our hearts; we have come out of the darkness of the world. Paul used the same analogy with the Ephesians:

> *For you were once darkness, but now you are light in the Lord. Walk as children of light (for the fruit of the Spirit is in all goodness, righteousness, and truth), finding out what is acceptable*

to the Lord....Therefore He says: "Awake, you who sleep, arise from the dead, and Christ will give you light" (Ephesians 5:8-10,14).

Christ is our light. In Him we see and know the Father. In Him we understand the truth of the gospel. In Him we have eternal life. In Him we also can receive revelation knowledge as God enlightens us in ways that are beyond the world's power and understanding.

A powerful example of this is found in the life of the prophet Elisha:

Now the king of Syria was making war against Israel; and he consulted with his servants, saying, "My camp will be in such and such a place." And the man of God sent to the king of Israel, saying, "Beware that you do not pass this place, for the Syrians are coming down there." Then the king of Israel sent someone to the place of which the man of God had told him. Thus he warned him, and he was watchful there, not just once or twice. Therefore the heart of the king of Syria was greatly troubled by this thing; and he called his servants and said to them, "Will you not show me which of us is for the king of Israel?" And one of his servants said, "None, my lord, O king; but Elisha, the prophet who is in Israel, tells the king of Israel the words that you speak in your bedroom" (2 Kings 6:8-12).

The king of Syria was extremely frustrated. Every secret plan he made against Israel was made known to Israel's king beforehand. So the Syrian king began looking for a traitor in his own camp, but a traitor was not the cause. Revelation knowledge was! The Holy Spirit revealed to Elisha all the plans of the king of Syria against Israel, and Elisha relayed the word to his king.

Such divine revelation knowledge is still a foreign experience to many churches and individual believers, but it is becoming more common. Today God is moving among His people in a mighty way, shaking us up and teaching us spiritual lessons that lift us high into "the heavenly places in Christ Jesus" (Eph. 2:6b). That is God's desire and purpose for us. Spiritual light is our destiny! When we are seated with Christ in the heavenly places, we can see and understand spiritual things.

Spiritual insight comes when we live by and walk in God's light. We become visionaries. That's what happened with Elisha. He saw through divine eyes what was going to happen and was able to prevent it by informing the king.

We really should not find this surprising. After all, we are talking about a God who can do anything; a God who can give visions in the night, dreams, and marvelous insight. You and I are living at only half our steam as believers in Christ. There is so much more for us to see and do when we get into the flow of what God is doing.

So it's time to get into the river and let God do whatever He wants to in and through you. Don't say, "I'm too old" or "I'm too young" or "I don't know enough." Instead, ask, "Lord, what can I do?" and He will show you. Make yourself available. Determine not to be contained any longer by spiritual blindness. Open your heart and mind fully to the light of Jesus and break out! Become the confident, victorious child of God that He wants you to be!

Chapter 5

Breakout From Fear

I once heard the story of a man who caused one of the greatest traffic jams in Sydney's history. He was going through the Sydney Harbour Tunnel–under the harbor–when he panicked and drove into the side of the tunnel wall. When a policeman came to the scene of the accident, he parked in the other lane, thereby holding up all the traffic waiting to go through the tunnel. Cars were backed up for miles and miles.

I'm sure this man is not the only person who has feared going through that tunnel. What if the concrete cracks and water starts pouring in while I am in there? What if an accident causes fumes to build up in the tunnel and asphyxiate me? What if I have a heart attack while I am in the tunnel and rescue personnel can't get to me? These and many other fears could cause a person to come to the entrance of the tunnel and stop, thinking, "I can't go in there."

Now, I drive through that tunnel twice a day, every day. I don't panic. I just do it. Why? I have faith that the people who designed the tunnel knew what they were doing, that they constructed the tunnel well and planned for the possible dangers.

Fear is always the absence of faith. It is one of the most powerful and effective devices that satan uses for containment. From the time Adam and Eve sinned in the Garden of Eden to this very moment as you read these words, fear has been an ever-present part of mankind's experience. It hounds, harrasses, and torments us, causing us to try to hide from whatever it is we fear.

We fear because our sin has separated us from God and left us subject to the wiles of the evil one. Now we don't know God or what we can expect from Him, life, or other people, so we hide like Adam and Eve hid from God because they were afraid. Such fear is a device of satan to destroy us. Multitudes of people, Christians and non-Christians alike, are held captive by every imaginable fear. Satan, the author of sin and the tempter, has lured them into his trap, and he's using every bit of power people let him have in their lives through fear.

Jesus came to "destroy the works of the devil" (1 Jn. 3:8) and fully accomplished His mission when He died on the cross and rose from the dead. Satan is a thoroughly vanquished enemy, although his ultimate destruction awaits the return of Christ and the last judgment. In the meantime, however, he still holds lost people under his control and uses many subtle devices—the greatest of which is fear—to contain unsuspecting and ignorant Christians.

So the way to overcome these schemes of the evil one is to understand that he is a defeated enemy and to live based on that knowledge. Indeed, the only power satan has over you as a believer is the power that you *allow* him to have. If you refuse to submit to him, he has no foothold in your life. James wrote, "Therefore submit to God. Resist the devil and he will flee from you" (Jas. 4:7). Everything in your old life that satan uses to accuse you has been crucified with Christ and you are no longer under condemnation because of it. Christ has set you free from satan's power. Likewise, every possibility in the future that could have a negative impact on your life is also subject to the great love Christ showed for you on the cross and the victory He won for you there. Paul affirmed this truth when he wrote,

> Everything in your life now and in the future is subject to the love, power, and authority of Jesus Christ.

> *Who shall separate us from the love of Christ? Shall tribulation, or distress, or persecution, or famine, or nakedness, or peril, or sword?...Yet in all these things we are more than conquerors through Him who loved us* (Romans 8:35,37).

Unfortunately, too many Christians do not live as though they have been set free, and indeed keep themselves in bondage by giving satan room in their thoughts. That's where the bondage of fear begins, in your thoughts. When you allow your thoughts to run rampant with all the "if onlys" and "what ifs," you suffer the ensuing torment. In effect, you cripple yourself.

Believers who are growing in the Lord, however, have daily opportunities to lay aside their fears and in faith embrace love. John wrote in his first epistle, "There is no fear in love; but perfect love casts out fear, because fear involves torment. But he who fears has not been made perfect in love" (1 Jn. 4:18).

Are you one of these believers? Are you being made perfect little by little through the love of the Lord Jesus Christ in your life? Or are you one of the many hundreds of thousands of people who are contained by satan through fear?

Dealing with all the fears that attack us in this world would require a book many times the size of this one. So let us consider what are perhaps the three most common fears for believers and unbelievers alike: fear of death, fear of loneliness, and fear of man.

Fear of Death

The fear of death is perhaps the most common fear that attacks men and women. Death is real. There is no escaping that fact. Both the experience of man and the witness of Scripture attest to it. Every person who has ever lived on the earth in past generations has died. The only exceptions are Jesus, who rose from the dead; Enoch, who "was not, for God took him" (Gen. 5:24b); and Elijah, who was taken into Heaven by a whirlwind (see 2 Kings 2:11). These exceptions were granted according to the sovereign purpose of God. Unless Jesus returns beforehand, every person now living or yet to be born will die. Scripture teaches us that "it is appointed for men to die once, but after this the judgment" (Heb. 9:27). Every human being has an appointment with death.

Fear of death is just as real as death itself. We know we can't escape death, yet we don't like to think about it. We push it to the back of our minds and then try all sorts of things to beat death or at least delay it for as long as possible. An incredible amount of time and money is expended each year on medical and scientific research to learn how to slow, halt, or even reverse the aging process. Millions of people are captivated by accounts of near-death experiences and visions of the afterlife. The concept of reincarnation found in Buddhism, Hinduism, and New Age beliefs has a growing appeal for many people. These interests are inspired by the fear of death and the desire to cheat it, if possible.

What is amazing is that so many *Christians* fear death. It is understandable for those who are without Christ and without hope to be afraid of dying and the "unknown" beyond it; but it should not be so for those of us who are partakers of the abundant life Jesus came to give! Yet multitudes of believers are afraid to die. I know this because over the years of my ministry I have talked and counseled with countless people who were gripped with fear upon receiving news of cancer or some other life-threatening disease or condition. Many others had such a tight grip on the things of this world (or the world had such a tight grip on them) that they feared the thought of leaving it all behind.

The writer of Hebrews said,

> *But we see Jesus, who was made a little lower than the angels, now crowned with glory and honor because He suffered death, so that by the grace of God He might taste death for everyone....Since the children have flesh and blood, He too shared in their humanity so that by His death He might destroy him who holds the power of death–that is, the devil–and free those who all their lives were held in slavery by their fear of death* (Hebrews 2:9,14-15 NIV).

Slavery. Isn't that a horrible, binding word? Lost humanity is enslaved by–bound by–fear of death. Through His death Jesus destroyed death and released from its power everyone who believes on Him. If you have trusted in Christ you have *already* defeated death; you have *already* passed from death into life. Eternal life is a *present reality* for you. Jesus said, "Most assuredly, I say to you, he who hears My word and believes in Him who sent Me *has* everlasting life, and shall not come into judgment, but *has passed* from death into life" (Jn. 5:24, emphasis added). Paul wrote to the Corinthians,

> *"Death is swallowed up in victory. O Death, where is your sting? O Hades, where is your victory?" The sting of death is sin, and the strength of sin is the law. But thanks be to God, who gives us the victory through our Lord Jesus Christ* (1 Corinthians 15:54c-57).

Moreover, the Spirit you received as a believer is not a spirit of fear. Writing to the church in Rome, Paul said, "For as many as are led by the Spirit of God, these are sons of God. For you did not receive the spirit of bondage again to fear, but you received the Spirit of adoption by whom we cry out, 'Abba, Father' " (Rom. 8:14-15). To Timothy, his spiritual son in the faith, Paul wrote, "For God has not given us a spirit of fear, but of power and of love and of a sound mind" (2 Tim. 1:7).

With all these scriptural truths as a foundation, why are so many Christians afraid to die? First, many Christians don't know what the Bible says about death. How then can all the Bible's assurances and promises of life and victory over death help in a time of need? They can't!

Wise counseling may be helpful for people who fear because of this lack of knowing and understanding what the Bible says about life and death, and the victory the Lord Jesus Christ won on the cross. This is particularly true for those Christians who have so underfed their souls that they are not even sure of their salvation. These believers naturally fear death because they feel insecure about their relationship with Christ.

I have witnessed the great joy and freedom that often come as a mature believer opens the Scriptures to an insecure believer and prays with him regarding his salvation. Nevertheless, if this immature believer does not continue to feed his spirit on the Word, if he doesn't hide it in his heart, if he doesn't build his life on its precepts, he inevitably sets himself up to be buffeted and beaten back and forth again by the storm waves of the world. In truth, he becomes, as James says, double-minded and unstable in all his ways (see Jas. 1:8).

On the other hand, Christians who have a solid foundation in God's Word have no fear of death because they are certain that life with Christ is their eternal destiny. When I nearly bled to death some years ago, I experienced the unbelievable peace that comes to those who know that they are secure in the hands of their Savior Friend. The peace I felt was so beautiful that I wished to stay there. Afterward, when my life was no longer in danger, I told Hazel, "If that's what dying is like, there is nothing to it. It's wonderful to be so at peace."

This peaceful experience is what God wants for all His children. He doesn't want you have doubts regarding your salvation and your life after death. John wrote in his first epistle,

> *And this is the testimony: that God has given us eternal life, and this life is in His Son. He who has the Son has life; he who does*

> *not have the Son of God does not have life. These things I have written to you who believe in the name of the Son of God, that you may know that you have eternal life, and that you may continue to believe in the name of the Son of God* (1 John 5:11-13).

A second reason many Christians fear death is because they lack a close walk with God born out of a rich prayer life. Such believers are completely unprepared when a life crisis suddenly arises. They feel the need to pray but find it difficult because they are filled with uncertainty. There is no strong relationship with their heavenly Father to assure them that He is in control and will carry them through the difficulties—or into the next life, if death is imminent. So when they do pray, it is more in desperation than from a lifestyle of prayer; more from fear than faith.

The first visit I ever paid to a hospital after my conversion was with members of the Salvation Army, and we went to see a lady who was dying with cancer. As I entered her room I was amazed to hear her singing the old gospel hymn, "Shall We Gather at the River." Her face was shining and she was bright and cheerful. Confident and unafraid, she looked forward to seeing the One who repeatedly said, "Fear not."

I saw this same peace when my wife and I visited a 16-year-old girl in the hospital dying with leukemia. It was a moving scene. Unafraid at the prospect of her death, this young woman told us that she believed in Jesus. Her faith in the Lord gave her peace, comfort, and confidence because she had come to understand for herself the truth of Psalm 23:4: "Yea, though I walk through the valley of the shadow of death, I will fear no evil; for You are with me; Your rod and Your staff, they comfort me."

A third reason Christians fear death is because their peace is being undermined by the knowledge of unconfessed sin in their lives. Spiritual maturity requires a daily turning from the pleasures of the flesh and to God in holiness. When this life of repentance and obedience is absent from a Christian's life, the assurance of salvation is weakened, or even lost. Here again counseling can help uncover the root of the fear of death. Then the sin can be confessed and forgiven, the containment in fear caused by the previously unconfessed sin can be broken, and faith can arise.

No believer has a reason to fear death. If you know the promises found in the Word of God concerning death, eternal life, and the victory Jesus won over death; if you are secure in your relationship with your Lord and your heavenly Father through prayer; if you live in brokenness and repentance, confessing your sins as the Spirit makes them known in your heart; and if you trust that God has done and will do all that He has promised, death has no hold on you. So even if you are killed tomorrow in a traffic accident or you drop dead tonight with a heart attack, you have no need to fear. Death has been swallowed up in victory, for when you die, your perishable body will drop away and your spirit will return to God, who gave the spirit to your body in the first place; and you will forever be with the Lord.

So why fear death? Remember that perfect love drives out fear. If you are walking with God, living a holy life, and seeking to love Him more and more, the devil cannot gain the victory over you unless you let him. The containment brought on by fear need not torment you. So, stand firm in what you believe. Don't worry or give in to fear of death. You have already passed from death into life (see 1 Jn. 3:14). Death has no victory.

Fear of Loneliness

Loneliness is a second great fear that grips mankind. It is one of the world's major problems today. That may seem hard to believe in a world of over six billion people, but it is the truth. There are multitudes of lonely people on the earth. This is particularly true for the elderly. The older people get, the more they fear that they will be left alone, that no one will visit them, and even that they might die alone in the house and no one will know about it.

Loneliness is not limited to the old, however. The greatest number of suicides occurs among young people, and many of these are because of loneliness. Frustration with life, low self-esteem, and problems with family, friends, teachers, and others have made these young people hate themselves and feel that they have nothing to live for. Lonely and afraid, they take their lives.

God knows that it is not good for us to be alone. We each need other people. That's why He gave the man the woman. That's why He puts us in families. That's why He likened the Church to a body where each member is needed. He is against loneliness.

The tragedy is that for many lonely people, particularly the elderly, loneliness is a lifestyle that has been unwittingly and unintentionally cultivated throughout a lifetime. Loneliness doesn't develop overnight. It comes from a lifestyle of shutting oneself off from reality; of becoming closed in through negative thinking. Lonely people become victims of the way they have lived. Some are lonely because they have spent their lives in negative thoughts, words, and attitudes. Others are lonely because they neglected to build good relationships when they had the opportunity to do so.

I know people who live alone yet are bright, happy, radiant believers in Christ whose greatest joy and pleasure is to talk with God and walk with Him. They are not lonely because God is their companion and ever-present friend. These people have also cultivated relationships with other people; they involve themselves in life beyond the confines of their own personal circumstances. I also know people who live alone and are quite lonely because they have allowed negativity and self-absorption to separate them from other people.

I myself am "elderly," but I don't feel like it. I haven't experienced old age. Neither am I lonely. I'm too busy. Even if my wife is taken before me, I will never be lonely because I am not a lonely person by nature and have never followed a lifestyle of negativity or isolation, which tend to produce loneliness. Indeed, I have built many wonderful relationships. More than that, I have built a solid relationship with my Lord and Savior, Jesus Christ. I find companionship in knowing Him and purpose in serving Him.

Faith is God's antidote for loneliness. Faith in God. Faith in His Word. Faith in His presence. The Scriptures are filled with people who delighted in living in the presence of God. Their reward was friendship with God.

In Isaiah 41 God says,

> *But you, Israel, are My servant, Jacob whom I have chosen, the descendants of Abraham My friend.* [Do you see that? God is calling Abraham His friend.] *You whom I have taken from the ends of the earth, and called from its farthest regions, and said to you, "You are My servant, I have chosen you and have not cast you away"* (Isaiah 41:8-9).

What a wondrous thought: to be chosen by God and not cast away! But look. It gets better.

> *Fear not, for I am with you; be not dismayed, for I am your God. I will strengthen you, yes, I will help you, I will uphold you with My righteous right hand* (Isaiah 41:10).

What a powerful, comforting, and encouraging Scripture for dealing with fear! Why should you fear loneliness or anything else if

God befriends you? In fact, this verse says four positive things to encourage you and remove your fear:

- *Fear not, for I am with you.* The positive power of God's presence is with you. If you name the name of Jesus, God is with you and for you. As Paul wrote to the Romans, "If God is for us, who can be against us?" (Rom. 8:31b) Why should you fear if God is for you? He is the great "I Am." There is no place you can go where you would be away from His presence or separated from His love.
- *Be not dismayed, for I am your God.* To be dismayed means to be discouraged or reduced to despair. The Lord is telling you not to be reduced to despair because He is your God. Do you know God like that? When some problem or trouble comes along, do you know where to turn? Don't be filled with discouragement. Rather turn to Jesus because He is the answer. He will comfort you. He will strengthen you. He will bless you. He is everything that you need. Even when you walk through the valley of the shadow of death, you need fear no evil because He is with you and He is sufficient for your every need. Nothing is too hard for Him, and He is always ready to aid those who are called by His name.
- *I will strengthen you.* God gives strength to those who run with Him. David wrote, "For by You I can run against a troop, by my God I can leap over a wall" (Ps. 18:29). That speaks of energy and life. Isaiah said, "But those who wait on the Lord shall renew their strength; they shall mount up with wings like eagles, they shall run and not be weary, they shall walk and not faint" (Is. 40:31). God gives you strength for every age and every need. That's fantastic! Just have faith and believe in God–be commited to Him–and God will strengthen you for every moment that lays before you.
- *I will help you, I will uphold you with My righteous right hand.* What more do you need if God is your help? If He upholds you, nothing can defeat you. The psalmist

> wrote, "God is our refuge and strength, a very present help in trouble" (Ps. 46:1). God has promised to help you and uphold you. He is your refuge and strength. With His constant presence there is no cause for fear or loneliness.

If then the message of the Scriptures is that there is no cause for loneliness, what can the Church do to confront this critical problem in our world today? How can the Body of Christ help people to break out of the containment of loneliness? One fundamental step is to teach people the importance of building relationships and to help them do it while they have opportunity. The church is a wonderful place for relationship building as members learn to enjoy other people and practice coming together, praying together, and working together toward common goals.

Of course, the most important relationship of all is one's relationship with God. Everyone needs to know that God loves him and wants to relate to him personally. This is why it is crucial that a local congregation teach clearly what the Bible says about God and man and the personal faith relationship with Him that God desires for every person. This is its primary mission. Such knowledge can go a long way toward alleviating the low self-esteem, self-hatred, negativity, and worthlessness that many lonely people feel. It can also help people to become rightly related to others and within themselves. Negative, defeating, and containing attitudes are replaced with a positive, healthy, and releasing outlook on life.

Another thing churches can do to counteract the fear of loneliness is to help the elderly break out of a "retirement" mentality. Society, particularly western society, generally focuses on retirement rather than on meaningful work. People are constantly challenged to save for retirement, to buy just the right insurance policies, and in other ways to prepare for retirement.

The Bible says nothing about retirement. Although the time does come when lessened energies and abilities may require a change from the daily work routine, elderly people still need to be involved and to make a positive contribution to society. The church is a perfect avenue through which this can happen. Ministries of visitation, intercession, and encouragement are all aspects of church life that can benefit from the assistance of retired persons. For example, a local congregation might start a grandparent program, where a child or teen and an older person are teamed up and share outings, visits, phone calls, or cards. Or older women might be paired with younger women–particularly new or young mothers–to support, help, and encourage them. The possibilities are really quite varied, and it doesn't really matter what program is used as long as the older person finds useful work to do that gives him or her the opportunity to focus on something or someone other than self.

If you are a retired person, just remember that you are never too old to do things for God. Keep healthy and fit to last the distance for God. Refuse to give place to the irritability and anger that elderly people are often noted for and look for ways to build up rather than criticize. If you choose such a lifestyle, you will find that others seek your company because they enjoy being with you and value your wisdom. This is surely an antidote for the loneliness that threatens to consume your later years of life.

Fear of Man

A third common fear is the fear of man. This fear, which has its roots in negative thoughts and living, cripples individual initiative and accomplishment both inside and outside the Church. It often holds a person back from being real because he can't be himself for fear that other people will not like him for who he is. Therefore he is afraid to launch out, to try something new, to shoot for his dreams. He is paralyzed, "For as he thinks in his heart, so is he" (Prov. 23:7a).

It is tragic that so many people in the Church of Jesus Christ are contained by the fear of man. Many believers never attain great spiritual heights simply because they are afraid of what people will say or think. The Book of Proverbs says, "The fear of man brings a snare, but whoever trusts in the Lord shall be safe" (Prov. 29:25). A snare is a trap. Fear of man traps and contains believers from becoming all they can be in the Lord, which just leads to more problems. Fear also reveals a lack of faith. The last part of Proverbs 29:25 promises safety from fear and the snare for those who trust in the Lord.

If you are going to be a breakout person, you must get beyond the fear of what other people think about you. Breakout people are not negative people. They have a healthy, positive self-image and are strong-minded. Firmly rooted in the truth of God's Word, they know who they are, where they are going, and how they are going to get there. Knowing that they have been lifted up and seated with Christ in the heavenly places, they have a positive attitude about life and a clear understanding of their strengths and weaknesses. They claim the words of Paul when he wrote, "I can do all things through Christ who strengthens me" (Phil. 4:13), and "Brethren, I do not count myself to have apprehended; but one thing I do, forgetting those things which are behind and reaching forward to those things which are ahead, I press toward the goal for the prize of the upward call of God in Christ Jesus" (Phil. 3:13-14).

The truth of these Scriptures is for you. If you are being contained by the fear of man, break out and say with David, "Whenever I am afraid, I will trust in You" (Ps. 56:3), and "In God I have put my trust; I will not be afraid. What can man do to me?" (Ps. 56:11) Faith is the antidote God has given you to banish fear. You can't move forward and stay where you are at the same time. Pressing forward requires faith, courage, and determination. You have to be willing to turn from the past, let go of your fears, and move ahead in the faith that the Lord will carry you through into the greater and higher things He has for you. The devil says, "Stay here. It's too scary out there." Jesus says, "If anyone thirsts, let him come to Me and drink. He who believes in Me, as the Scripture has said, out of his heart will flow rivers of living water" (Jn. 7:37b-38).

As a child of God, you are not made for bondage and withdrawal out of fear, but for faith, freedom, and victory. Be careful, then, to heed the words of the writer of Hebrews:

> *Therefore we also, since we are surrounded by so great a cloud of witnesses, let us lay aside every weight, and the sin which so easily ensnares us, and let us run with endurance the race that is set before us, looking unto Jesus, the author and finisher of our faith, who for the joy that was set before Him endured the cross, despising the shame, and has sat down at the right hand of the throne of God* (Hebrews 12:1-2).

Choose now to run well the race God has put before you, laying aside the fear that would hinder you from running freely.

Chapter 6

Release of Human Emotions

One afternoon some years ago when I was doing a crusade in New Zealand, a local pastor called me concerning a particular woman he had counseled that afternoon in his office. She was so crippled with arthritis that she could barely walk. Although an unbeliever, she had heard that I had a healing ministry and that miracles of healing had been occurring at the meetings. Her husband had brought her to this pastor to see what could be done. During their visit the pastor received a word of knowledge regarding her condition. He told her, "Your arthritis is the result of the bitterness and hatred you feel toward your brother who hurt you. They have become a cancer in your soul, crippling your spirit just as the arthritis now cripples your body."

The woman, completely amazed that this pastor knew about her brother, confirmed his word by relating to him how her brother had been extremely mean to her and had hurt her very deeply. She had nursed that hurt and bitterness for years and it dominated her thoughts and her life.

The pastor then asked her, "Do you really want to be free from this illness?" When she replied that she did, he said, "You must go to your brother and tell him that you are genuinely sorry for holding a grudge of bitterness toward him. You must forgive him for the hurt he caused you and ask him to forgive you for hating him, ignoring him, and refusing to speak to him all this time."

The woman did just what the pastor told her and the next night was sitting near the front in my crusade meeting, still crippled and unable to walk. When I went to pray for her, I asked her if she had ever received Christ as her Savior. She said, "No, but I want to." I led her to the Lord right there and then told her that I was going to pray for her and God would heal her. So I laid my hands on her and prayed, and within a couple of minutes the power of God went right through her body. She jumped to her feet and began running up and down the aisle completely released and healed by the power of God.

I believe to this day that this woman never would have experienced healing if she had not been willing to forgive and seek forgiveness. No matter what else she tried, she would have remained bound in her body by the crippling condition of her spirit. When she broke out of her sin and unforgiving spirit into the light of Christ's love, she also received physical healing.

Certainly not every illness has a spiritual or emotional cause behind it, but I believe many do. Health care professionals have recognized for years that the majority of mental illnesses have an emotional rather than a physiological or biochemical cause. Emotional stress also has been linked as a causative factor in many physical ailments. For these reasons we cannot afford to ignore the emotional element of human personality as a significant factor in containment and breakout.

Breakout Through Forgiveness

An unforgiving spirit is perhaps the greatest single hindrance to Christians breaking out into the deeper, higher life in Christ. I fear that the modern Church, particularly in the West, takes far too lightly the entire matter of forgiveness or unforgiveness and its consequences. God's Word certainly does not take it lightly. In fact, the entire message of the Scriptures is a record of God's forgiving, redemptive activity toward humanity in providing a way of salvation and reconciliation.

Forgiveness Is in God's Nature

Why is forgiveness so important? The Bible makes it clear that forgiveness is in the very nature of God. Anything that characterizes God is important to His children because we are supposed to be like Him. Forgiveness of sin lies at the very heart of the gospel message: Without forgiveness there is no salvation.

The Bible is full of statements and examples of the forgiving nature of God. Consider these words from the Psalms:

> *For You, Lord, are good, and ready to forgive, and abundant in mercy to all those who call upon You* (Psalm 86:5).
>
> *If You, Lord, should mark iniquities, O Lord, who could stand? But there is forgiveness with You, that You may be feared* (Psalm 130:3-4).
>
> *You have forgiven the iniquity of Your people; You have covered all their sin* (Psalm 85:2).

David knew from personal experience the forgiving nature of God:

> *Blessed is he whose transgression is forgiven, whose sin is covered....I acknowledged my sin to You, and my iniquity I have not hidden. I said, "I will confess my transgressions to the Lord," and You forgave the iniquity of my sin* (Psalm 32:1,5).

Jesus Himself gave the most powerful demonstration of the forgiving nature of God when He spoke from the cross, "Father, forgive them, for they do not know what they do" (Lk. 23:34b). Only One who had already extended forgiveness in His heart toward His enemies could ask the Father to forgive them. Bruised, beaten, spat upon, scorned, reviled, and crucified, Jesus nevertheless regarded those who hated Him with love, compassion, and forgiveness.

God's forgiveness is readily available, but it is *not* automatic. It is given only to those who seek after it and ask for it in a heart attitude of humility, confession, and repentance. John the apostle wrote, "If we confess our sins, He is faithful and just to forgive us our sins and to cleanse us from all unrighteousness" (1 Jn. 1:9). God Himself said to Solomon, "If My people who are called by My name will humble themselves, and pray and seek My face, and turn from their wicked ways, then I will hear from heaven, and will forgive their sin and heal their land" (2 Chron. 7:14). God's forgiveness is conditioned on our confession and repentance.

Jesus illustrated this clearly in His parable of the Pharisee and the publican (see Lk. 18:10-14). Both men went to the temple to pray. The Pharisee's "prayer" was a bragging session on himself as he reminded God how good he (the Pharisee) was. The publican, however, couldn't even look God in the eye and was able only to cry out, "God, be merciful to me a sinner!" Jesus said that the publican was the only one who went home right with God.

God's Mercy and Forgiveness Are for You

Perhaps you can recall an event or a broken relationship in your life where you erred so greatly that you have wondered, or even denied, that your sin could be forgiven. The good news is that God's faithfulness to forgive sin applies to you. You are not beyond the reaches of His mercy. Indeed, the prophet Isaiah testifies,

> *He* [God] *has not dealt with us according to our sins, nor punished us according to our iniquities. For as the heavens are high above the earth, so great is His mercy toward those who fear Him; as far as the east is from the west, so far has He removed our transgressions from us. As a father pities his children, so the Lord pities those who fear Him* (Psalm 103:10-13).

What comforting words! God promises to take pity on us and remove our transgressions from us. Then, as the writer of the Book of Hebrews testifies, we can draw near to God "...with a true heart in full assurance of faith, having our hearts sprinkled from an evil conscience and our bodies washed with pure water" (Heb. 10:22). This is possible because we "enter the Holiest by the blood of Jesus, by a new and living way which He consecrated for us, through the veil, that is, His flesh" (Heb. 10:19b-20).

> No one...
> nothing...
> is beyond the reaches of God's love, mercy, and forgiveness.

Indeed, no one is beyond the reaches of God's mercy–not the thief on the cross, the murderer on death row, or the father who fails his children. All who acknowledge their transgressions and confess the evil they have done are assured of forgiveness. This means that no matter what you have done, how you have failed, or where you have been, God's forgiveness is a present reality in your life if you have confessed your sin. Truly He no longer even remembers the wrongs you have done (see Is. 43:25; Heb. 10:16-17).

Hallelujah! What freedom! You don't have to live in containment from your past sin. You can live in the fullness of God's abundant mercy. Just be careful to confess your sin, to turn from continuing in it, and to pass the same mercy you receive on to those who sin against you. Also, don't forget to forgive yourself, because you'll find it impossible to live in the light and joy of God's mercy if you are continually bombarding yourself with feelings of guilt and regret. If God's forgiven you, there's no reason why you should continue in unforgiveness toward yourself.

Forgiveness Is Required of Us

Christ the Lord has Himself set the example for us in forgiveness. We who claim Him as Lord and Savior are to do as He has done, forgiving others their wrongs against us just as He has forgiven us. In a very real way, our receiving forgiveness depends on our willingness to forgive others: "For if you forgive men their trespasses, your heavenly Father will also forgive you. But if you do not forgive men their trespasses, neither will your Father forgive your trespasses" (Mt. 6:14-15).

On another occasion Jesus explained the importance of forgiveness with a parable that was prompted by a question from Peter: "Then Peter came to Him and said, 'Lord, how often shall my brother sin against me, and I forgive him? Up to seven times?' Jesus said to him, 'I do not say to you, up to seven times, but up to seventy times seven' " (Mt. 18:21-22). Jesus then told the story of a servant who owed his master a fortune and was to be sold, along with his family, in order to pay the debt. When the servant pleaded for mercy, his master graciously forgave the debt. The servant promptly went out and accosted a fellow servant who owed him a few dollars and had him thrown in a debtor's prison despite the man's pleas for patience. Upon hearing of this, the master brought the first servant before him and berated him for his refusal to forgive his fellow servant as he had been forgiven. The master then turned the servant over to the torturers until he paid his debt in full. Jesus ended the story with a warning: "So My heavenly Father also will do to you if each of you, from his heart, does not forgive his brother his trespasses" (Mt. 18:35).

Forgiveness is *serious business* with God! Nothing kills a church, stops a believer's spiritual growth, or quenches the Spirit faster than an unforgiving spirit. It is *impossible* to harbor unforgiveness in your heart and be in a right relationship with the Lord. Unforgiveness is iniquity (sin) that separates you from God. The psalmist said, "If I regard iniquity in my heart, the Lord will not hear" (Ps. 66:18). Any sin, including unforgiveness, that you harbor in your heart (refuse to confess) blocks your communication with God and grieves and quenches the Spirit in your life. John wrote in his first letter,

> *If someone says, "I love God," and hates his brother, he is a liar; for he who does not love his brother whom he has seen, how can he love God whom he has not seen? And this commandment we have from Him: that he who loves God must love his brother also* (1 John 4:20-21).

Forgiveness is active, not passive, and its goal is reconciliation and restoration of fellowship and harmony. Thus a spirit of forgiveness means that you will not only freely extend forgiveness to others but will also actively seek forgiveness from anyone you have wronged. It does not matter whether you have been wronged or you are the one who wronged another person; you are responsible to seek reconciliation. Jesus spoke of this in His Sermon on the Mount when He said,

> *Therefore if you bring your gift to the altar, and there remember that your brother has something against you, leave your gift there before the altar, and go your way. First be reconciled to your brother, and then come and offer your gift* (Matthew 5:23-24).

Seeking reconciliation is more important than worship! In fact, it is impossible to truly worship when you know that you have an unresolved conflict with a brother or sister in Christ. To worship God without seeking to reconcile the conflict is hypocrisy.

It is easy then to understand why lack of forgiveness is such a powerful source of containment. If you desire to break out to the deeper and higher things of Christ but find yourself bound and unable to get free no matter how hard you try, maybe you should look deep into your heart and ask the Lord to show you if there is an unforgiving spirit lurking there. Is there anyone whom you have not forgiven or from whom you need to ask forgiveness? Is there any unresolved conflict between you and another person? Take care of it right away. You will never experience the abundance of life in the Spirit, the fullness of joy, or the satisfaction of victory until you do. Remember too that the power to forgive lies beyond yourself; it is possible only through the Lord's presence and power.

Breakout From Hurt

Closely related to a lack of forgiveness is the hurt that many Christians harbor inside, hurt that comes from what another person has done or said to them. This buried hurt contains these Christians, sometimes for years, because they don't know how to break away from the pain. Left untreated, the hurt deepens into a festering sore, and like a cancer in the soul becomes a continuing problem that impacts all of life.

Such hurts may wound not only the person who was originally hurt but also those people with whom the wounded person interacts. This happens as the wounded person expresses his or her bad attitudes to other people and consequently hurts them. They in turn pass on to others the condemning statements caused by their hurt, and the chain goes on and on.

You may wonder how you can break out from the emotional hurt that contains your life. It is important first to take care of any unforgiveness that is hidden within you, since emotional hurt often is a doorway through which an unforgiving spirit or root of bitterness gains access to your heart. Resolving the forgiveness issue and reconciling with the person or persons involved many times takes care of most, if not all, the hurt.

If the hurt remains or is deep-seated, you must then determine not to live in the past any longer, dwelling on or brooding over the pain. Make a conscious decision to move forward and get on with life, claiming the presence and power of Christ to do so. Repeating and claiming scriptural truths and promises is a powerful balm for doing this. The Book of Psalms contains dozens of promises that reveal and release God's power to heal emotional pain. Consider these verses:

> *But let all those rejoice who put their trust in You; let them ever shout for joy, because You defend them; let those also who love Your name be joyful in You* (Psalm 5:11).

> *You will show me the path of life; in Your presence is fullness of joy; at Your right hand are pleasures forevermore* (Psalm 16:11).

> *The Lord is my rock and my fortress and my deliverer; my God, my strength, in whom I will trust; my shield and the horn of my salvation, my stronghold* (Psalm 18:2).

> *The Lord is my strength and my shield; my heart trusted in Him, and I am helped; therefore my heart greatly rejoices, and with my song I will praise Him* (Psalm 28:7).
>
> *The Lord will give strength to His people; the Lord will bless His people with peace* (Psalm 29:11).
>
> *For His anger is but for a moment, His favor is for life; weeping may endure for a night, but joy comes in the morning* (Psalm 30:5).
>
> *My flesh and my heart fail; but God is the strength of my heart and my portion forever* (Psalm 73:26).
>
> *The Lord is my strength and song, and He has become my salvation* (Psalm 118:14).
>
> *Those who sow in tears shall reap in joy* (Psalm 126:5)
>
> *He heals the brokenhearted and binds up their wounds* (Psalm 147:3).

Even as you seek to heal the hurts you carry, you must also be sensitive to recognize the people whom *you* have hurt, people who may be contained and bound up because of what you said or did.

Years ago when I was a young Christian and not yet in the ministry, I had a major argument with my pastor. I said some very hateful and judgmental things that hurt him very deeply. On top of it all, the things I said were incorrect. I had wronged him terribly.

Some time later, after he had been transferred by the Salvation Army from New Zealand to London, England, I found myself going through spiritual and emotional difficulty. I was contained by the negative and harsh spirit I had shown toward my former pastor. Deeply convicted by the Holy Spirit, I wrote a letter to him asking for his forgiveness and apologizing for my unkind words and unChrist-like spirit.

Hurt, bitterness, and unforgiveness are deadly.

Soon I received an amazing letter from him. He wrote, "Frank, your letter was like a balm in Gilead to me. It came at a most wonderful time. This week we attended the coronation of Queen Elizabeth, but it was even more wonderful to receive your letter. Certainly my wife and I both forgive you and thank God that you must feel good within your own soul."

Hurt, bitterness, and an unforgiving spirit are also deadly dangers for churches. They cause strife, division, contention, confusion, and animosity and often divert the church's attention from its mission of evangelism and ministry. If satan can get us fighting among ourselves, he has won 90 percent of the battle. Countless churches have split and even closed their doors over such things, leaving hundreds of wounded, hurting people in the dust.

Dissension and division in the Church is ungodly; they are of the devil. The Bible warns against them repeatedly. Paul wrote to the Romans, "Now I urge you, brethren, note those who cause divisions and offenses, contrary to the doctrine which you learned, and avoid them" (Rom. 16:17); and to the Corinthians, "Now I plead with you, brethren, by the name of our Lord Jesus Christ, that you all speak the same thing, and that there be no divisions among you, but that you be perfectly joined together in the same mind and in the same judgment" (1 Cor. 1:10), and "For you are still carnal. For where there are envy, strife, and divisions among you, are you not carnal and behaving like mere men?" (1 Cor. 3:3)

Pastors and other church leaders who are sensitive and Spirit-led can often relieve these pressures and tensions through solid biblical teaching, resulting in therapeutic cleansing and healing within the Body of Christ. This is God's way. His Word is powerful and He honors it when it is preached, taught, and believed in faith.

When you obey the voice of God in your heart, the balm of the Spirit goes to work, healing hurts, repairing divisions, and reconciling you with brothers and sisters of faith with whom you have disagreed. There is no greater way to honor and glorify God than to allow Him to manifest His loving, healing, forgiving, gracious nature in you and through you. When you do this, He is magnified before the world.

Breakout From Discouragement

Another of satan's powerful weapons of containment is discouragement. For any number of reasons, the people of God easily become discouraged with life. Lengthy or frequent illness, family strife, job stress, financial hardship, legal difficulties, unemployment, harsh criticism, moral or ethical failure–any of these can lead to deep discouragement. In the midst of a difficult situation, it is easy to focus squarely on the problem and feel that there is nothing else in life *except* that problem. Discouragement then becomes a repeating, self-defeating cycle as discouragement feeds discouragement. And the more you are discouraged, the more you lose touch with reality—spiritual reality.

The solution to discouragement is taking your eyes off the problem and focusing them instead on Jesus, who can take away your problem. No matter how great your trouble, Jesus is greater still. No matter how deep your despair, Jesus is deeper still. No matter how strong the forces against you, Jesus is stronger still. Jesus told His disciples, "These things I have spoken to you, that in Me you may have peace. In the world you will have tribulation; but be of good cheer, I have overcome the world" (Jn. 16:33). John encouraged the readers of his first epistle when he wrote, "You are of God, little children, and have overcome them, because He who is in you is greater than he who is in the world" (1 Jn. 4:4). John's phrase, "have overcome them," refers to the false prophets and the spirit of antichrist that are loose in the world. Jesus has overcome them all; through His presence and power in you, so can you.

Another powerful weapon against discouragement is the Word of God itself. If you get into the Bible and seriously read and study it, you soon discover that you really do have a God who is greater than the world; one who loves you and dearly desires that you live in union and fellowship with Him. This knowledge is in itself a potent antidote to discouragement. As Paul said in his letter to the Romans, "If God is for us, who can be against us?" (Rom. 8:31b) The prophet Jeremiah also recorded God's attitude toward His children:

> *For I know the thoughts that I think toward you, says the Lord, thoughts of peace and not of evil, to give you a future and a hope. Then you will call upon Me and go and pray to Me, and I will listen to you. And you will seek Me and find Me, when you search for Me with all your heart* (Jeremiah 29:11-13).

I know for myself that I couldn't keep up with my schedule and responsibilities if I didn't maintain my own soul through reading the Scriptures and through prayer. That's where I find the strength to keep doing everything that God has set before me to do, despite the setbacks and disappointments that are part of life. How can I remain discouraged when I know that God is for me, desires for me a future of peace and hope, listens to my prayers, and makes Himself available to me?

The problem for many Christians, however, is that satan has contained them so that Bible reading and prayer are not part of their daily life. Then when discouraging situations and events pile in upon them they have no resources with which to fight the depression that threatens to consume them.

If you are one of the many who continually fight depression and discouragement and are overwhelmingly wearied by the demands of life, listen again to the words of Jesus,

> *Come to Me, all you who labor and are heavy laden, and I will give you rest. Take My yoke upon you and learn from Me, for I am gentle and lowly in heart, and you will find rest for your souls. For My yoke is easy and My burden is light* (Matthew 11:28-30).

Jesus' promise is that you will find rest for your soul. The promise is contingent, however, upon your going to Him and letting Him ease your heavy burden. In other words, discouragement can be either a constant weight pulling you down or a temporary inconvenience overcome through faith in the Word and the power of God—the choice is yours.

The apostle Paul evidently learned this secret of dealing with life's difficulties. If anyone had human reason for discouragement and despair, it was the apostle Paul. He endured hardship, suffering, persecution, and difficulty everywhere he went. I'm sure that at times it would have been very easy for him to give up and quit. He never did, though, because he had his heart and his eyes in the right place: on Jesus. This is quite evident in his second letter to the Corinthian church, where he reveals his attitude toward the discouragement and difficulty in the world:

> *We are hard-pressed on every side, yet not crushed; we are perplexed, but not in despair; persecuted, but not forsaken; struck down, but not destroyed–always carrying about in the body the dying of the Lord Jesus, that the life of Jesus also may be manifested in our body. For we who live are always delivered to death for Jesus' sake, that the life of Jesus also may be manifested in our mortal flesh....For our light affliction, which is but for a moment, is working for us a far more exceeding and eternal weight of glory, while we do not look at the things which are seen, but at the*

things which are not seen. For the things which are seen are temporary, but the things which are not seen are eternal (2 Corinthians 4:8-11,17-18).

Paul found a way to look beyond and move past the difficulties he faced. You must do the same. Discouraging things happen in life; you can't escape that. What you can change is how you respond to them. You must choose whether you will live in discouragement and defeat—which is just what the devil wants you to do—or look beyond your circumstances to the reality of God's loving care and protection and the power He has given you to overcome. In Jesus you have everything you need. Jesus is your strength, Jesus is your power, Jesus is your wisdom and encouragement to rise above everything negative that the world throws your way. Refuse to be sucked in by the beguiler's schemes!

Breakout From Failure

Personal failure is another of satan's lures to entrap Christians in discouragement. Whether it is failure on the job or at home, a moral or an ethical defeat, the emotional aftermath can leave the victim thinking: *I'm a loser. I can't do anything right. I'll never amount to anything in life.* Those are the kind of things I heard as a boy from my old headmaster in school. Had I listened to him and accepted his judgment of me, I might have ended up as a drunk dying in a filthy gutter somewhere. Praise be to God that He had other plans for me!

To overcome the discouragement that follows a failure, you need to know how to come back quickly instead of spending long periods of time in negativism. You know what I mean...the orgies of pessimism that both reflect and embody the sense of hopelessness that runs rampant after a personal failure. The only way that I've discovered to overcome this disappointment and self-condemning attitude is to go to the Word of God. I've made that a habit. I always spend much time reading the Bible, but I am particularly careful to read the Word when I'm discouraged because of some relationship or experience where I failed.

Reading the Word has a gloriously cleansing and purifying effect on my soul. Not only does this reading cleanse me but it also feeds my soul and gives me new strength. Where I thought I couldn't go on, the Spirit of God through the Scriptures revived me and gave me the will to try again. Evidently I'm not the only one who has found this to be helpful because not long ago I heard a preacher advise his congregation to run to God, not to negativism and a sense of defeat, when they had failed.

Running into negativism just puts you into a tailspin of failure that often is quite difficult to pull out of. Then you are precisely where the enemy of your soul wants you to be: wallowing in defeat, self-pity, guilt, and self-condemnation. The best way to respond to failure is to recognize your failure, go to the Word of God, ask God to forgive you, and get on with life. Otherwise you will get stuck at that point of failure, and there's no need for this because *our Lord is the God of second chances!*

Consider Moses, for example. Born a Hebrew, nurtured early in the faith of his people, and raised and educated in the house of Pharaoh, Moses was being prepared to fulfill God's purpose as the deliverer of the Israelite people. Suddenly, he brought it all crashing down, or so it seemed. His premature attempt to reveal himself as the deliverer backfired when his murder of an Egyptian overseer forced him to flee Egypt into a 40-year exile in the wilderness of Moab. Working as a shepherd over the flocks of his father-in-law, Moses appeared to have utterly failed.

However, the God of second chances met Moses one day in a burning bush and Moses' life was forever changed. The 80-year-old fugitive murderer/shepherd, armed with the presence and power of God and a renewed commission from God, returned to Egypt and led the Israelites out of slavery. Now that's quite an accomplishment for a man who may have given up on himself! The key is that God had not given up on him.

Bold, brash Simon Peter is much like Moses. On the night before Jesus' crucifixion he impulsively pledged that he would follow Jesus even to the death, but within a few hours that same Simon Peter had publicly denied three times that he even *knew* Jesus. This failure broke Peter and might have destroyed him...had it not been for the God of second chances. A few days later the Lord met Peter on the shore of the Sea of Galilee and asked him three times, "Simon, do you love Me?" Three times Peter answered that he did, and three times Jesus responded, "Feed My sheep." (See John 18; 21.) Restored through forgiveness and empowered by the Spirit, Peter the denier became Peter the proclaimer as he boldly preached Christ before men. Peter may have given up on himself during those dark days after his denial, but God never did. With mercy and love

Jesus redeemed what He had seen in Peter long before. He restored the rock, on whom the Church would be built (see Mt. 16:18).

Are you haunted by the guilt or shame of a personal failure? Do you feel that there is no hope for you now? Have the bold dreams you once had for yourself or your family drifted away to where they seem hopelessly out of reach? Have you tried–and failed–once too often and fear you lack the courage or will to try again? Take heart, my friend. Don't let satan contain you any longer in the bondage of hurt, discouragement, or failure. You were created for more than that. The God of second chances (and third, fourth, and fifth...) stands before you with His strong right hand reaching down to lift you up "into the glorious liberty of the children of God" (Rom. 8:21b). Choose today to take God's hand and rise above the fears that have threatened to consume you. He is more than able to free you from every snare.

Chapter 7

Filling Up by Pouring Out

My first visit to India really opened my eyes. Never before had I seen such unbelievable poverty. In Bombay, little children were lying in the streets dying, many of them so weak from malnutrition that they lacked the strength even to brush away the flies that ran in and out of their mouths. People walking along the streets would step right over them as if they weren't there. Not a soul bent down to help them. The very sight of these terrible conditions made me cry.

Then a man named Graham Truscott took me to the booming church he pastored in the heart of the city. While sitting with me on the platform during a meeting, he asked me, "Frank, what do you notice about this congregation?"

After studying the people for a few moments I replied, "They all look exceedingly happy."

"What else?"

"Well, they all seem to be pretty well-dressed."

"Exactly. All these people came off the streets. A few years ago they had no homes. They lived under pieces of cardboard or pieces of sack, even under old newspapers. Some of them slept in drains. Without money, they had to scavenge around for bits of food to eat. Frank, you are looking at a miracle."

What had happened to change poor, starving people into a happy, prosperous congregation? There is one significant answer: tithing. Graham taught them to tithe. How could they tithe if they had no money? They learned to tithe on what they had. At one time they were fed from a food pool, being given carrots and other vegetables

> God honors you when you honor Him with your tithe and offerings.

and such. Graham taught them to take a tenth of what they received and tithe it to the Lord: a tenth of their carrot, a tenth of their onion, etc.

As the people learned this and practiced it, bringing their tithes together, they began to feed more people and receive more food. Soon, as their consistency in tithing was demonstrated, they suddenly began to find jobs where before jobs had been impossible to get. Before long, they were able to buy decent clothes, and over a period of time, they started to prosper. Their prosperity was exceedingly wonderful. Because they honored God, God honored them. They obeyed the Word of God, and God fulfilled His Word.

This is a lesson that churches of the western world sorely need to learn. It amazes me that western Christians, who are among the most materially prosperous in the world, are also the most contained believers in the world when it comes to money, possessions, and giving. Many of us seem to have a major problem either understanding or obeying God's Word regarding our attitudes and disposition toward money and material possessions. Generally speaking, we have a pretty dismal track record in stewardship and in giving in faithful obedience to the work of God's Kingdom. I believe that this is a major reason for why we have not seen more miracles, more people saved, and a greater impact of the Church on the world.

God or Mammon?

As recorded in the four Gospels, Jesus speaks more on money and material possessions than He does on any other single subject. Perhaps this is because nothing else has greater potential to divide people and to become an idol standing between them and God. Jesus understood well the allure of worldly wealth for sinful men and time after time warned against being seduced and trapped by it. One of His most familiar teachings on the subject is found in the Gospel of Matthew:

> *Do not lay up for yourselves treasures on earth, where moth and rust destroy and where thieves break in and steal; but lay up for*

> *yourselves treasures in heaven, where neither moth nor rust destroys and where thieves do not break in and steal. For where your treasure is, there your heart will be also....No one can serve two masters; for either he will hate the one and love the other, or else he will be loyal to the one and despise the other. You cannot serve God and mammon* (Matthew 6:19-21,24).

Jesus plainly stated, "You cannot serve God and mammon," yet it is amazing how many people try anyway. There is room in our hearts for only one god and that *must* be the Lord. John wrote, "Do not love the world or the things in the world. If anyone loves the world, the love of the Father is not in him" (1 Jn. 2:15). We cannot have divided love or divided loyalties.

Two instances in the Gospel of Mark illustrate the contrast of attitudes toward money and, consequently, toward God. One day a man ran up to Jesus and asked Him what he must do to inherit eternal life. Jesus reminded him of the commandments of God. When the man assured Jesus that he had observed those commandments all his life, Jesus then said, "One thing you lack: Go your way, sell whatever you have and give to the poor, and you will have treasure in heaven; and come, take up the cross, and follow Me" (Mk. 10:21b). This was not the answer the man expected: "But he was sad at this word, and went away sorrowful, for he had great possessions" (Mk. 10:22). Jesus went on to tell His disciples how hard it is for a rich person to enter the Kingdom of Heaven. His point was that the *love* of riches gets in the way.

In the second instance,

> *...Jesus sat opposite the treasury and saw how the people put money into the treasury. And many who were rich put in much. Then one poor widow came and threw in two mites, which make a quadrans. So He called His disciples to Himself and said to them, "Assuredly, I say to you that this poor widow has put in more than all those who have given to the treasury; for they all put in out of their abundance, but she out of her poverty put in all that she had, her whole livelihood"* (Mark 12:41-44).

The value was not in the amount of the gift but in the love that lay behind it. The poor widow's gift showed that she loved God and knew that all that she had was from God and belonged to Him. Her gift also showed her faith that God would provide for her needs. The rich man's wealth was an idol that separated him from God. The widow's "two mites" were a means by which she worshiped and honored God.

Giving to Reach the World

Before Jesus left His disciples and ascended into Heaven, He gave them some clear instructions. Matthew closes his Gospel with these words:

> *And Jesus came and spoke to them, saying, "All authority has been given to Me in heaven and on earth. Go therefore and make disciples of all the nations, baptizing them in the name of the Father and of the Son and of the Holy Spirit, teaching them to observe all things that I have commanded you; and lo, I am with you always, even to the end of the age. Amen"* (Matthew 28:18-20).

Early in the Book of Acts, Luke records these words of Jesus: "But you shall receive power when the Holy Spirit has come upon you; and you shall be witnesses to Me in Jerusalem, and in all Judea and Samaria, and to the end of the earth" (Acts 1:8).

Both of these passages show Jesus speaking power and authority to His Church to enable us to represent Him and act like Him on earth. He has both commanded and empowered us to be His witnesses throughout the earth. This is the Church's mandate, our very reason for existing. We must go, we must send, and we must provide the means for those who go. The apostle Paul wrote,

> *How then shall they call on Him in whom they have not believed? And how shall they believe in Him of whom they have not heard? And how shall they hear without a preacher? And how shall they preach unless they are sent?* (Romans 10:14-15a)

The Church is the Body of Christ in the world commissioned to tell the world about Him and to make disciples of all the nations. This requires commitment, hard work, preparation, prayer, and *money*. We cannot proclaim the gospel of Jesus Christ without money. We cannot do the work of the Kingdom if we are not willing to pay the price, literally.

Yet many, many churches throughout the world, and particularly in the West, fail to do all that they want to do or feel led to do because they lack the funds to pay for it. Studies have shown that in most churches 80 percent of the work and virtually all the funding are contributed by 20 percent of the members. The number of tithers in most churches is about the same percentage. Consider the implications of this: If every believer tithed–gave 10 percent of his gross income to the Lord through his local church–every church would have all the money it would need to carry on any ministry it could imagine. Instead of skimping and scraping to get by, local congregations would have the resources to do whatever God wanted them to do. As it is now, most churches don't have near enough money to fund every vision or ministry God lays on His people's hearts.

My wife and I have learned the joy not only of tithing, but of giving offerings. Yet my wallet is always full. We never run out. Often I am surprised and delighted by the ways God chooses to bless us. One Sunday morning a young boy came and stood in front of me with his hands behind his back. He said to me, "Pastor, I've got a gift for you. There's something in my hand. Which hand do you think it is in?" I guessed the right hand and was right. When the boy took his hand from behind his back, he handed me a brand-new ten dollar note. He said, "I've saved this up for you." How fantastic! God blessed us through a little boy.

I was quite moved by the boy's gift. I gave him a kiss and told him, "What you've done is great. Thank you. I promise you that God will give more back to you than you have given to me." Some people might say that I shouldn't have taken the money from the boy. I disagree. He would have been upset had I not taken it. Also, why would I want to rob him of the pleasure of giving it to me? His delight in giving was evident on his face.

Many Christians have not learned this delight in giving. They have a blind spot when it comes to money. The bottom line is unbelief: Failing to practice what God has said in His Word. The Scripture says that "God loves a cheerful [lit. 'hilarious'] giver" (2 Cor. 9:7b), yet we give sparingly and grudgingly from a sense of duty. God says, "You shall have no other gods before Me" (Ex. 20:3), yet we make idols of our possessions and our money, saying, "This is mine and nobody is going to tell me what to do with it." Such an attitude is direct rebellion against God. Satan has locked us into the world's beliefs about money and giving so that we can't see God's laws concerning wealth and the blessings of obeying them. True biblical belief is belief that is put into practice.

Hearing and understanding the truth of God's perspective on money and giving is essential for several reasons. First, it is God's nature to give and therefore must be our nature too. Second, everyone will be called to give an account to God of their stewardship of the resources He has given them. Third, God wants us to prosper, and giving is the key to prosperity. Fourth, giving is an incredible God-given privilege and opportunity.

Giving Is in God's Nature

When we think about the nature of God, many things come to mind: gracious, merciful, compassionate, kind, loving, righteous, just, holy. Another aspect of God's nature is that He loves to give. Making the sun to rise on the evil and the good, and sending rain on both the just and the unjust (see Mt. 5:45), God particularly enjoys giving good things to His children. James wrote, "Every good and every perfect gift is from above, and comes down from the Father of lights, with whom there is no variation or shadow of turning" (Jas. 1:17). Truly, God is the most excellent giver, having given us all things, the most precious of which are His Son (see Rom. 6:23; 8:32) and the grace and faith to receive the Son (see Eph 2:8-9). What greater gift could there be?

If God is willing to give this much to save sinners, how could we doubt His willingness to give all good things to His children? Paul stated it well when he wrote,

> *What then shall we say to these things? If God is for us, who can be against us? He who did not spare His own Son, but delivered Him up for us all, how shall He not with Him also freely give us all things?* (Romans 8:31-32)

Notice the phrase "all things." God's desire is to give us not a few things, not some things, but all things–spiritual and material. He wants to bless us abundantly. This is not a "name it and claim it" prosperity theology that looks on God as someone to be manipulated to give us wealth. Not at all. It is the giving of a loving Father who wants nothing but the best for His children, and who is committed to doing everything–even to the point of giving His sinless Son to die for our sins–to give us this abundant, successful, victorious life.

We Are to Be Givers

Clearly, then, the Scriptures reveal God's giving nature; and because He is a consistent, excellent giver and He created us to be like Him (see Gen. 1:26-27), He wants us to have the same spirit of generosity. Jesus certainly displayed this generous spirit of giving during His time on earth. Truly He lived a lifestyle of giving. In this, as in everything else, He is our great example and teacher. There are five specific commands regarding giving that Jesus gave to His disciples. These reflect the kind of attitude we are to have toward giving.

1. *Give to all who ask.* Jesus said, "Give to everyone who asks of you. And from him who takes away your goods do not ask them back" (Lk. 6:30). A few years ago my wife and I were in London for some meetings. It was winter and bitterly cold. One evening we braved the weather to go to a supermarket. A young man sat shivering in the cold outside the supermarket with a sign asking for money to buy a meal. I thought about him all the time we were inside. I felt the Spirit in me telling me to give the young man some help. When we went back outside, I gave him $200. He couldn't believe it. I could hardly believe it myself. The joy on that man's face was indescribable. As for me, I felt like skipping back to the hotel. I was so liberated and free of that cursed money that didn't belong in my pocket. It belonged to the hungry young man. God wanted him to have it. The truth is that I never even missed it because like He always does, God honored my faithfulness. Truly I have never regreted giving from my purse because in my life God has been proven to be faithful to His Word.

2. *Give as you have received.* Jesus told His disciples, "Freely you have received, freely give" (Mt. 10:8b). There is a divine cycle at work here: God gives, you receive; you give, others receive; God gives, you receive; you give, others receive.... God has given to you so that you can give to others. If you fail to give, you break the cycle, thereby depriving yourself—and those to whom God intended that you woul give—of His blessings.

3. *Give to meet the needs of people.* One example of this is in Luke 9:13 when Jesus instructed His disciples to feed the people. He then proceeded to bless the five loaves and two fish, afterwhich He gave them to the disciples to distribute to the crowd of over 5,000 people. In this and many other instances, Jesus taught by example that believers are to have compassion for the needs of others and to give from their resources to meet those needs. Some might say, "But I need that money. I can't pay my own bills if I'm always taking care of others." Do you remember the divine cycle mentioned in the previous paragraph? God gives so that you can give; and when you give, He

gives you more. Indeed, when you give God your meager resources in faith and obedience by giving them to a person in need, God honors your gift and returns it to you. More than that, He multiplies it so that both you and the one to whom you have given are blessed.

4. *Give and you will receive abundantly.* Jesus said, "Give, and it will be given to you: good measure, pressed down, shaken together, and running over will be put into your bosom. For with the measure that you use, it will be measured back to you" (Lk. 6:38). Did you catch the meaning of that last sentence? You cannot *receive* abundantly if you are not willing to *give* abundantly because you have not been given God's resources in order to hoard them for yourself. Rather, you have been blessed so that you can give. God stands ready to pour out more on you as you are faithful to give out what He has already provided. When you give willingly, God's blessings flow. You can never outgive God.

5. *Give to the poor.* Jesus used the occasion of dining in the house of a Pharisee to give these instructions: "But when you give a feast, invite the poor, the maimed, the lame, the blind. And you will be blessed, because they cannot repay you; for you shall be repaid at the resurrection of the just" (Lk. 14:13-14). God has always been a champion of the poor, the orphan, the widow; everyone who has no one to plead their cause or defend them. If they are close to God's heart, then they need to be close to yours as well.

Stewards of God's Bounty

How do we develop such an attitude that we consistently live by these teachings of Jesus? The answer lies in understanding that we are stewards managing God's wealth. If the Church is to succeed in carrying the gospel to the whole world in our generation (or even in the next), we must break out of our containment where money is concerned. We must learn to grip our possessions loosely, recognizing that all we have belongs to God, that He has made us stewards over His money and possessions, and that we are accountable to Him for how we use them.

The Scriptures make it abundantly clear that everything we have belongs to God. Therefore He has a right to talk to us about our finances. The question is, will we listen and obey His requirements for stewardship? Will we believe what He says?

Sadly, Christians are rarely as giving as God is. Instead of giving with the same generosity that God shows to His children, many

Christians tend to hold on to their money and material wealth. This often results in problems that could have been avoided had we understood our role as stewards and taken our responsibility seriously.

The requirements for our stewardship begin with the tithe. The tithe is basic: ten percent of our gross income. This is the portion God designated that we set aside for His Church, although He owns the whole of our wealth.

> *"Bring all the tithes into the storehouse, that there may be food in My house, and try Me now in this," says the Lord of hosts, "if I will not open for you windows of heaven and pour out for you such blessing that there will not be room enough to receive it"* (Malachi 3:10).

So the tithe is the basic minimum that God requires us to give to Him. An offering is anything we give to God above and beyond the tithe. Tithing is basic obedience; an offering shows love and spiritual growth beyond the most basic requirement.

It would be safe to assume, then, that a lack of tithing reveals much more than an inability to manage our money well. Truly it reveals a spiritual immaturity, a meagerness of godliness. Godliness means being God-like. God wants us to be godly. He has created us in His own image and likeness (see Gen. 1:26-27) and expects us to live accordingly, reflecting that divine image in our lives. So if you want one measure of how Christ-like or God-like you are, look at your finances and how much you give to God.

God wants you to be wise about your money. He doesn't want you to be burdened with it. Thus, the more you try to hold on to your money, the less likely you are to be successful, both financially and in other areas of your life. Indeed, if you are not giving a tithe to the Lord, you are mostly likely struggling to make ends meet and may even have amassed great debt.

One day you will have to give an account to God of how you used the resources He lent you. This is clearly revealed in the parable of the talents as told in the Gospel of Matthew. This story tells of a man who was about to travel to a far country. Before he left, he called each of his servants in and gave them a portion of his property to steward while he was gone. When he returned, he asked each for an accounting of what they had done with his money. Two of the servants had doubled their master's assets. To each the master said, "Well done, good and faithful servant; you were faithful over a few things, I will make you ruler over many things. Enter into the joy of your lord" (Mt. 25:21b). But the third servant returned only what had been given to him. So the master said to him,

> *"You wicked and lazy servant, you knew that I reap where I have not sown, and gather where I have not scattered seed. So you ought to have deposited my money with the bankers, and at my coming I would have received back my own with interest. Therefore take the talent from him, and give it to him who has ten talents. For to everyone who has, more will be given, and he will have abundance; but from him who does not have, even what he has will be taken away"* (Matthew 25:26b-29).

Notice that the wicked steward lost even the little he had been given. So it is with us. When we steward well whatever resources God entrusts to us–be they plentiful or meager–we open the door for God to give us more to steward. The prosperity God gives to us is based on what we do with what He has already given us.

Poverty or plenty depends on what you do with whatever God gives you.

This is why so many believers have financial problems and struggle with money. They live from paycheck to paycheck either because they don't understand God's principles of stewardship and giving or because they have chosen not to obey them.

God Wants to Prosper You

I wish that every child of God really understood, believed, and chose to obey the truths concerning God's divine order for giving and receiving. God wants you to prosper. This is clearly revealed in the Scriptures. Indeed, the Old Testament contains numerous examples of God prospering those who were faithful to Him: Abraham, Joseph, Moses, David, and Solomon, to name a few. In the New Testament, John wrote, "Beloved, I pray that you may prosper in all things and be in health, just as your soul prospers" (3 Jn. 2).

God's will for you is that you prosper and enjoy health. If you want to enjoy the prosperity that God wants to give, you must believe God's Word and take it seriously. This begins with tithing. When you start tithing, you will begin to see God prospering you. His blessings poured into your life will increase.

Paul describes these blessings in this way: "Now may He who supplies seed to the sower, and bread for food, supply and multiply the seed you have sown and increase the fruits of your righteousness, while you are enriched in everything for all liberality..." (2 Cor. 9:10-11). If God means what He says here, and I know that He does, the Christian Church around the world is like a great, sleeping giant that is beginning to stir. God is waking up His Church. He is stirring us to fulfill our responsibilities as stewards of His gifts—both the material blessings we have and the great gift of the good news of Jesus Christ. When the Church is fully awake with the spiritual fire to boldly proclaim and to cheerfully, sacrificially give, watch out! The whole world will be transformed!

That transformation must begin with you. Study the Word and find out what resources God has made available to you:

> *That the God of our Lord Jesus Christ, the Father of glory, may give to you the spirit of wisdom and revelation in the knowledge of Him, the eyes of your understanding being enlightened; that you may know what is the hope of His calling, what are the riches of the glory of His inheritance in the saints, and what is the exceeding greatness of His power toward us who believe, according to the working of His mighty power* (Ephesians 1:17-19).

Look at what God wants to give you: wisdom, revelation knowledge, enlightened understanding, the riches of His glorious inheritance, and the exceeding greatness of His power. Anyone who has these things could certainly be considered prosperous! Verse 18, in particular, speaks of the eyes of your understanding being enlightened. You have spiritual eyes through which you can receive supernaturally imparted understanding of divine wisdom. This wisdom includes knowing how and when to give as a steward of the Lord's resources. When you learn this, God can fulfill His heart to prosper you. You give and He blesses.

Discover the Joy of Giving

All this leads to the truth that giving is an incredible God-given privilege and opportunity. Truly, learning to give is one of the most liberating things that can happen to you. I learned to give from my mother. She was a tremendous giver. She gave cheerfully from her heart, seeing it as an act of worship, part of the holy work God had commissioned her to do. She never gave for the purpose of receiving, but on many occasions, God blessed her because she had blessed others. So much did her lifestyle of giving impact me that I used my first paycheck to buy a gift for her.

God wants you to succeed, not fail. He cheers you on to victory in life, not defeat. He has planned that all aspects of your life will prosper and be in good health. This includes your finances. Because He is your gracious heavenly Father, He also wants you to have fun and to find fulfillment while you are prospering and succeeding. The divine cycle of giving and receiving is one way He fulfills that intent for your life.

There is joy in giving liberally to bless others as God has blessed you. As I mentioned earlier when telling the story of the man who sat outside the London supermarket, there is something positively invigorating about giving. Perhaps this is true because God created us to give; and when we give, we tap into the joy that showing concern for the needs of others brings—joy so great that it inspired Jesus to endure the shame of the cross that we might be saved (see Heb. 12:1-2). Such joy in giving is a matter of faith.

Jesus trusted His Father to be true to the plan He had laid out. He went to the cross believing that He would again take His rightful place in Heaven. This faith in His Father enabled Him to stay on the cross even in that moment when His Father forsook Him because of our sin. You must give with the same attitude. The prosperity you trust God for may not be immediately evident when you give faithfully, obediently, and sacrificially out of love for the Lord, but you must trust God to be faithful to His Word—even when the circumstances would seem to indicate otherwise. Such giving shows that you trust your heavenly Father and rely on Him—and Him alone—to provide for your needs.

> Faith gives when reason would say to hold on to everything you can get.

The contrary is also true. If you refuse to give, believing that you don't have sufficient resources to share, you reveal that your heart has not been perfected in love and that you do not believe that God will take care of you.

> *No one has seen God at any time. If we love one another, God abides in us, and His love has been perfected in us. By this we*

> *know that we abide in Him, and He in us, because He has given us of His Spirit...Love has been perfected among us in this: that we may have boldness in the day of judgment; because as He is, so are we in this world* (1 John 4:12-13,17).

A lack of faith cuts you off from God's provisions and blessing. Faith shown through giving, on the other hand, releases His storehouses of blessing so that you have more and more and more to give.

So if cash is tight, that's precisely when you need to give; and as you do, you will discover both the wonderful grace that is given to those who trust the Lord and the joy of seeing your faith rewarded so that you can give again. I have never regretted giving something away. Indeed, the joy of giving has so captivated me that I am always giving things away.

I pray that you might discover the same joy. Choose today to break out of the "poverty" syndrome. Resolve in your heart to give to the Lord a tenth of your income, no matter how small your income may be. God doesn't want you to live on the bread line or to not know where your next dollar or meal is coming from. He yearns to prosper you in all ways—both spiritually and materially. So make the choice today to break out of material bondage by tithing your income to the Lord and by giving freely to those in need from the resources God has entrusted to you. You won't be sorry. Rather, you'll be overwhelmed by the goodness and the provision of the Lord.

Chapter 8

The Power of Release

It is one thing to *talk* about breakout; it is quite another to *do* it. The fundamental difference between a Christian who is joyful, mature, growing, and victorious and one who is not is that the former has made the choice to break out no matter the cost or the obstacles. A breakout Christian has discovered the power of God for walking in the Spirit and for living in victory. Contained Christians are either ignorant of the higher purpose of God for their lives and the power He makes available to them, or they have decided that the cost in sacrifice and inconvenience is too high to pay. Either way, they are missing out on the tremendous blessings and high plane of living that are theirs as children of God. It is like sipping gruel in the kitchen while the rest of the family enjoys a sumptuous feast in the banquet hall.

From the day Jesus instituted His Church He made it clear that it would be an organism of power. When Simon Peter said of Jesus, "You are the Christ, the Son of the living God" (Mt. 16:16b), Jesus commended Peter for his faith, then said, "...you are Peter, and on this rock I will build My church, and the gates of Hades shall not prevail against it" (Mt. 16:18). With these words, Jesus indicated that His Church would not be a defensive body digging in to withstand the attacks of the enemy, but an offensive army that would storm the very gates of hell.

Just before He ascended, Jesus spoke of the power that would enable the Church to fulfill its mission: "Behold, I send the Promise of My Father upon you; but tarry in the city of Jerusalem until you are endued with power from on high" (Lk. 24:49). "But you shall receive power when the Holy Spirit has come upon you; and you shall be witnesses to Me in Jerusalem, and in all Judea and Samaria, and to the end of the earth" (Acts 1:8).

God has provided His children with a full array of spiritual assets for breakout power: weapons for waging war against the enemy, gifts for edifying the Church and equipping the saints for ministry, and endowments that help individual believers grow and mature in Christ-likeness.

Spiritual Weapons for Breakout

Although we live in a world controlled by satan, we as believers are not under his power. God has redeemed us to be, as Paul says, "more than conquerors through Him who loved us" (Rom. 8:37b). God has provided a way for us to be winners. Not leaving us to our own devices in the fight against sin and evil, He has made available to us a formidable arsenal of weapons with which to do battle. When we take up these weapons in faith and in the knowledge that the battle is the Lord's rather than ours (see 2 Chron. 20:15-17), we experience victory as He triumphs in and through us.

The first and most important weapon we have for breakout is the blood of Jesus. His blood covers our sin and frees us forever from sin's bondage (see Eph. 1:7; Rev. 1:5). The blood of Jesus satisfies our guilt before God and opens the way for us to enter boldly into the Most Holy Place of intimate fellowship with Him (see Eph. 2:13; Heb. 10:19). Jesus' blood removes all claims of satan to accuse us before God. Whenever we mention the blood of Jesus, the devil trembles with fear and the demons leap backward. They can't stand before the power of the blood of Jesus. There is a wonderful old gospel hymn that expresses this beautifully:

> Would you be free from your burden of sin?
> There's power in the blood, power in the blood.
> Would you o'er evil a victory win?
> There's wonderful power in the blood.
> There is power, power, wonder-working power
> In the blood of the Lamb.
> There is power, power, wonder-working power
> In the precious blood of the Lamb.[1]

1. Lewis E. Jones, "There Is Power in the Blood." Public Domain.

A second potent weapon closely linked to the blood of Jesus is the mighty name of Jesus. God Almighty has invested in that name all the power and authority of the Godhead so that when even the weakest saint uses the name of Jesus in faith, he has the same power as though Jesus were physically standing beside him. By speaking the name of Jesus you can overcome temptation, forcing satan to flee; you can cast out demons, bringing deliverance to those in bondage (see Mk. 16:17; Acts 16:18); and you can pray with confidence and power, knowing that the prayer in Jesus' name (according to His will) will be answered (see Jn. 14:2-14; 15:16; 16:24).

> The name of Jesus is as powerful as the physical presence of Jesus standing beside you.

I certainly have found this to be true in my life. Again and again I have witnessed the power in the name of Jesus. I had a young fellow call me one night and say, "Please come down, please come down to my motel." A married, Christian man from another church, where a revival was going on, he had taken a girl off the street and brought her into his motel room. When he told me on the phone what he had done, he said, "I haven't committed a sin, but I brought her into my room, and when I got her on the bed, I was so ashamed of myself and such conviction grabbed a hold of me. I know that I have a devil in me. Come down and cast out this devil."

I happened to know this fellow, his hotel was a long way off, and it was late at night so I said, "That demon's been in you a long time. It can wait until the morning. You be at my office at nine o'clock tomorrow morning." The next morning when he came, I got two other pastors and we went up to my office. What happened next was unlike anything I had ever seen. This was a dignified young man, but when we started to minister to him, he took to us. First he sent the three of us flying. I ended upside down with my glasses off; one of the other pastors ended up under a table; and the third went flying over the table and landed on his head on the other side. Next the young man charged straight into the wall with his head down and made weird noises, but there was not even a bump on his head. Then he rushed back again. By this time I had recovered myself, and I stood up and shouted, "In the mighty name of Jesus Christ, you devil, I command you to come out of him." Immediately the young man did a backward flip and landed on his back, which was my salvation because he was coming right for me. As he lay there, I proceeded in the all-powerful name of Jesus to cast the devil out of him with the help of my brothers, and we set him free. Today he is a very successful pastor.

The power and the name of Jesus are but two of the spiritual weapons we have as Christians. The apostle Paul gives an excellent picture of the other weapons in our arsenal. Inspired by the familiar sight of a well-equipped Roman foot soldier, he wrote to the Ephesians:

> *Finally, my brethren, be strong in the Lord and in the power of His might. Put on the whole armor of God, that you may be able to stand against the wiles of the devil. For we do not wrestle against flesh and blood, but against principalities, against powers, against the rulers of the darkness of this age, against spiritual hosts of wickedness in the heavenly places. Therefore take up the whole armor of God, that you may be able to withstand in the evil day, and having done all, to stand. Stand therefore, having girded your waist with truth, having put on the breastplate of righteousness, and having shod your feet with the preparation of the gospel of peace; above all, taking the shield of faith with which you will be able to quench all the fiery darts of the wicked one. And take the helmet of salvation, and the sword of the Spirit, which is the word of God; praying always with all prayer and supplication in the Spirit, being watchful to this end with all perseverance and supplication for all the saints* (Ephesians 6:10-18).

A critical key in breakout power is to remember that your strength and might are in *the Lord* and not in yourself. On your own you are easily defeated by your spiritual adversaries; in Christ, you overcome.

The weapons that Paul lists here provide complete protection for both offensive and defensive actions:

The belt of truth. Just as a soldier's belt served to hold the various pieces of equipment he needed, so also the truth as revealed by God is the fundamental source for the equipping of the saints.

The breastplate of righteousness. A soldier's breastplate protected his heart and other vital organs. In a similar manner, righteousness protects your heart, or inmost self, because it is the quality that makes you just and upright before God.

The shoes of readiness. With shoes on his feet a soldier was ready to march for many miles to engage in battle. Likewise, the saints of God are prepared to go anywhere and do anything for their King, and to boldly proclaim the gospel of His Kingdom. Isaiah says, "How beautiful upon the mountains are the feet of him who brings good news, who proclaims peace, who brings glad tidings of good things, who proclaims salvation, who says to Zion, 'Your God reigns!' " (Is. 52:7)

The shield of faith. The large Roman shield warded off the blows of the enemy and provided, especially when linked with others, an invincible phalanx under which the soldiers could advance. Likewise, faith protects you from the corrupting influence of the world and other types of demonic attack and gives you the protective cover under which you advance against the enemy.

The helmet of salvation. Like the helmet that protected the soldier's head, where his mind and reasoning capacity were located, so salvation covers and protects you in your individual personhood. You are lifted up by the sure hope of your salvation. In fact, Paul referred to it just this way in another letter: "But let us who are of the day be sober, putting on the breastplate of faith and love, and as a helmet the hope of salvation" (1 Thess. 5:8).

The sword of the Spirit, the Word of God. The short broadsword was the Roman soldier's chief weapon for close hand-to-hand combat. God's Word was the primary weapon Jesus used during His temptation by the devil in the wilderness. It defends against error, heresy, and the lies of the enemy; turns back the legions of darkness; and tears down the strongholds of satan. The writer of Hebrews described it this way: "For the word of God is living and powerful, and sharper than any two-edged sword, piercing even to the division of soul and spirit, and of joints and marrow, and is a discerner of the thoughts and intents of the heart" (Heb. 4:12).

Prayer. Although there is no parallel here to a soldier's armor, the importance of prayer in the spiritual arsenal of the saints of God cannot be underestimated. Just as soldiers in the field must look to their commanders for orders, so prayer opens up for you the way to know the heart of God and to receive revelation of His will. Just as soldiers are trained to care for and watch out for one another on the field, so prayer affords a way to support and cover others as you advance together in spiritual warfare.

Don't sit around helplessly in "Camp Containment"; put on your armor, pick up your weapons, and boot satan out of your life.

God has equipped you to be in His "breakout army"; has set you free from sin, death, and the pull of the world by His Spirit; and has commissioned you to "preach good tidings to the poor...to heal the brokenhearted, to proclaim liberty to the captives, and the opening of the prison to those who are bound; to proclaim the acceptable year of the Lord" (Is. 61:1b-2a). If you're not seeing this fruit in your life, it's time to put on your armor and send satan packing. Don't sit around helplessly in "Camp Containment"; in faith, courage, and confidence use all the weapons that God has made available to you and break out to new and higher ground!

Spiritual Gifts for Breakout

In addition to weapons for the battle, the Lord has also given us many and varied spiritual gifts–resources for the ongoing work of building up the Church and equipping the saints for ministry and service. The greatest of these gifts is the Holy Spirit Himself who now dwells in every believer and is the source and giver of all the other gifts.

Across the full spectrum of the Christian Church there exists much disagreement, debate, confusion, and ignorance on the subject and substance of the spiritual gifts. As a result, many Christians have a very limited understanding of spiritual gifts and the relevance that the gifts have to their lives as believers. This ignorance is a source of containment for them because by not exercising their gifts, they impede the process of reaching their full potential in Christ. The problem is compounded by the fact that today, even in Pentecostal circles, there is not enough basic teaching on gifts being done in local churches. It is important to understand what the gifts of the Spirit are, how they operate, and why they were given to the Church.

The first thing you need to remember is that the gifts of the Holy Spirit are for ***you****. They have been given to* ***every believer****, not only to ministers of the gospel or a specially chosen elite.* Since the Holy Spirit, who is the source and giver of the gifts, dwells in every believer, He has given gifts to you. Paul wrote to the Corinthians regarding the Spirit's role concerning gifts:

> *There are diversities of gifts, but the same Spirit. There are differences of ministries, but the same Lord. And there are diversities of activities, but it is the same God who works all in all. But the manifestation of the Spirit is given to each one for the profit*

> *of all....But one and the same Spirit works all these things, distributing to each one individually as He wills* (1 Corinthians 12:4-7,11).

Paul says that "the manifestation of the Spirit is given to each one" and that the Spirit distributes "to each one individually as He wills." So then, every believer, including you, has received gifts from the Spirit. They are given not for the exclusive benefit of the individual believer, but "for the profit of all." Paul's list of nine gifts emphasizes, as does the discussion that follows, this corporate function of the gifts: the word of wisdom, the word of knowledge, faith, gifts of healing, the working of miracles, prophecy, discerning of spirits, different kinds of tongues, and interpretation of tongues (see 1 Cor. 12:8-10). In the verses that follow (vv. 12-27), Paul stresses the importance of each individual member to the proper working of the whole Body. When any one member does not function, the entire Body suffers.

The word of knowledge, for example, is a remarkable tool for any Christian to use. Sometimes I get amazing perceptions in the Holy Spirit. I recall one meeting where I was walking up the aisle, and immediately I knew that there was somebody right by me that had a hiatal hernia. So I said, "Who here has a hiatal hernia?" To my surprise, six or eight people lifted their hands. They were all sitting together, and they all looked at each other in amazement. So I laid hands on them and prayed for them and they were healed.

In another meeting a number of years ago, I pointed toward the back of the auditorium, which was filled with 400 to 500 people, and said, "There is a lady back there who is experiencing a problem. I'll tell you what is inside your purse, which will identify you from everybody around you. When the meeting is over, I want you to come see me and the pastor of this church." After the meeting the woman came to see me, as I had asked her to do, and emptied her purse on the table, revealing all the stuff—everything—that I had mentioned. It was incredible. The pastor and I then ministered to her regarding her problem.

When I lived in New Zealand, I had a friend who came from Australia to visit us. They landed in Auckland and rented an old car to drive down to Wellington, in the southern part of the island, where we were living. It was a hot summer day, so they decided to stop at Lake Taupo for a swim. After their swim, my friends got into the car and resumed their journey. When they had traveled about 100 miles, they realized that they had lost a valuable ring.

Now, anyone who knows that lake knows that it is very cold. Obviously, the cold water had shrunk her finger and the ring had slipped off while they were swimming. When they got to our house, they told me what had happened. Immediately I could see the ring on the bottom of the lake. So I told my friend, "When you go back, remember the place you came out of the water. Then step off so many yards (I don't remember how many yards it was) out into the water and look down. You will see the ring sitting on the white sand."

Some time later I received a phone call. Excitedly, my friend said, "Guess what?" I said, "I don't have to guess, I know. You did what I told you to do and you found the ring." He said, "I did exactly what you said, and sure enough, when I looked around, there it was lying on the bottom of the lake."

These examples of the gift of knowledge are but a few of many I have received over the years, and I know that such experiences are not peculiar to me. Others too receive these amazing perceptions in the Holy Spirit. Indeed, such knowledge received through the Spirit of God is available to every believer. Whether or not you have used this gift of the Spirit does not change the fact that you can see things in the Spirit if you are careful to keep your spirit attuned to God's Spirit.

Very often this flow in the Spirit is tied to your consistency in prayer and Bible study. God says, "I can trust this man (I can trust this woman) because he (she) reads My Word, studies My Word, and allows My Word to be in his (her) heart." So the believer who is founded in the Word of God is able to perceive things and know things that are not discerned by the natural mind.

If you want to be a breakout Christian, you must learn to walk in this and other giftings of the Spirit. This happens as you recognize and accept your giftedness by the Spirit and in God's power develop and exercise your gifts in the ministry of your local church. As you find and take your appropriate place within the Body of Christ and function there, the whole Body benefits. In the same manner, breakout churches must be careful to release *all* their members—men, women, *and* children—to operate in their gifts, helping them to discover, develop, and use them under the leadership and power of the Spirit.

The second essential truth regarding the gifts of the Holy Spirit is that they were given for specific purposes. The first purpose is to help bring people to Christ. Spiritual gifts are involved in preaching the gospel with the authority and power to bring about confession, repentance, and faith in the hearers. Manifestations of the more visible gifts—signs and wonders—confirm the truth of the gospel message proclaimed by preaching. Teaching gifts build up the members in their knowledge and understanding of the truth, and administrative gifts help organize and streamline the Body to function more effectively, thereby reaching more people with the gospel.

I have regularly used the gifts of the Spirit in my evangelistic ministry. Once when I was preaching in India, a very well-dressed young man came down the aisle toward me, swearing and cursing at me at the top of his voice. With his finger pointed out at me, he said, "What right, you so-and-so, do you have to come and preach to us? We don't need you and your so-and-so religion." I was taken aback because the meetings had been great, with many people giving their lives to Jesus, and the Indian Christians had treated me quite well. Immediately I lifted my heart to God because the young man's eyes were literally flashing with anger. The moment I called on the name of the Lord in my heart, I had authority, and I put my finger out toward him and said, "I am here because the Holy Ghost brought me here."

Then God did an amazing thing. He gave me a word of knowledge about the young man, something I could not possibly have known apart from the Spirit of God because I didn't know anybody in India. God told me the name of the exact place where he was that morning. When I said, "At eight o'clock this morning, you were at such-and-such a place," my accuser reeled backward and started to go backward up the aisle. As he retreated, I went after him, telling him one thing after another that the Lord was revealing to me through the word of knowledge. By this time everybody was looking at us. After all, there were only three or four white people among hundreds and hundreds of Indians, so the eyes of all these Indians were on me as God was working supernaturally.

Finally, the young man dropped into an empty seat, lifted up his hands, and started to shout at the top of his voice, "Jesus Christ, I never believed in You. I thought that You were a fake... I repent and give myself to You." Then and there he gave his life to Jesus. Hallelujah!

But that's not the whole story. Afterward I discovered that he had a knife in his pocket that he had intended to get out and use to stab me to death in front of everybody. When he first came up the aisle toward me, I noticed that his hands were clenched at his sides. Later, when he gave his testimony, he said, "I could not unclench my fists or bend my elbows until I fell into the seat and surrendered myself to Jesus. Then I began to praise Him and to call on His name."

Not all gifts of the Spirit take such a spectacular form, and when they do, the gift is never given for the gift alone. This is why some churches run into problems when they begin celebrating the gifts for their own sake and as an end in themselves rather than as God-given resources for reaching people. When this happens, the church is on a fast track to error, excess, and irrelevance. We cannot, we *must not*, reserve the gifts of the Spirit for ourselves alone or abuse them by exercising them for the wrong reasons, such as simply to draw attention to ourselves or to show others how "spiritual" we are. Either error will grieve and quench the Spirit of God.

Another purpose for the Spirit's giving of spiritual gifts is to build up the Church and to equip believers for ministry and service. Paul addressed this in his letter to the Ephesians:

> *And He Himself gave some to be apostles, some prophets, some evangelists, and some pastors and teachers, for the equipping of the saints for the work of ministry, for the edifying of the body of Christ, till we all come to the unity of the faith and of the knowledge of the Son of God, to a perfect man, to the measure of the stature of the fullness of Christ* (Ephesians 4:11-13).

God wants the Church to grow to full maturity in Christ, being unified, knowledgeable, well-grounded in faith, and filled with the Spirit so that we can fulfill His commission to make disciples of all the nations. To help us achieve this well-rounded growth, Christ gave to His Church apostles, prophets, evangelists, pastors, and teachers. It is not God's purpose that these persons do all the work and ministry of the Church, but that they help to equip the full Body for ministry. To this end, these leaders are to establish local churches on a firm spiritual foundation; to strengthen them in the faith; and to teach, train, challenge, and equip every member to do the work. When this happens, each member of the Body can claim his giftedness through the presence of the Holy Spirit and take his place as a fully functioning member of the Body of Christ.

With all these resources God has given you there is no reason, no excuse, for you to remain contained in your personal spiritual life or in your ministry through your local church. Don't let satan keep you in ignorance. Ask the Lord to reveal your gifts and to open avenues of opportunity for you to begin exercising them. Then break out and claim the full heritage God has given you!

Spiritual Endowments for Breakout

An endowment is a natural capacity, power, or ability. In the unredeemed condition, all people are spiritually dead and lack spiritual endowment. Breakout is impossible. When you come to Christ, however, you receive a new nature that is endowed with the spiritual capacity to understand spiritual truth and to activate the spiritual power to live in a manner that is pleasing to God. The apostle Paul refers to this as putting off "the old man which grows corrupt according to the deceitful lusts" and putting on "the new man which was created according to God, in true righteousness and holiness" (Eph. 4:22,24). This new spiritual capacity, made possible by the grace of God, flows over, through, and out of our lives in the anointing of the Spirit and is brought to effect in our lives through faith.

Grace. Grace is God's unmerited, unearned favor. It is given to us so that we can be free. Grace means not giving us what we *do* deserve (judgment, condemnation, punishment) and giving us what we *do not* deserve (forgiveness, righteousness, freedom, life). Jesus said, "Therefore if the Son makes you free, you shall be free indeed" (Jn. 8:36). Freedom is God's heart and desire for us. He loves us, cares for us, and wants to release us to ever higher levels and planes of living. His grace alone makes this possible.

God's grace is not a one-time, once-for-all impartation; it is a continually flowing river. From the moment you came to Christ, you have been living under God's grace; and it will continue to cover you throughout eternity. If God ever removed His grace from over you, you would be finished. So every day you live, wherever you go, whatever you do, you are covered by the wonderful grace of God.

Being under God's grace frees you from sin's bondage and opens up a vast new world of potential for you. God wants you to realize that you have seeds of greatness within you, possibilities beyond your natural comprehension. You certainly have not attained all you can attain. Maybe that's part of God's plan: you always have goals to shoot for. I am convinced that by God's grace every person can lift himself to a higher realm of life, faith, and experience.

I remember from some years ago in my church in Sydney a young man whose experience illustrates this very principle. He was good-looking and had a lovely young wife and two small children.

However, his hair was long and unkempt, and he and his family were always dressed in poor, shabby clothes. Despite the fact that he was quite bright, they lived on the edge of poverty. He was contained, not living up to his potential.

One day I said to him, "Do you know that you are living way below God's standard for you? He wants so much more for you." He looked quite surprised. I continued, "The sad thing is that you have great possibilities. You are very capable and yet you are living just from hand to mouth. You don't have a steady job and yet you are talented. You are gifted."

"What could I do?" he asked.

I said the first thing that came into my head. "You could be a great salesman. Clean yourself up, get your hair cut, sell the junk around your house that you don't need, and buy yourself a nice suit and some new shoes. Then go out and get a job. You could sell cars. They would even give you one to drive. Your whole standard of living would change. You could have a better house, and your wife and kids could wear nice clothes."

"Do you really think I could do that?"

"I know that you can if God puts it in your heart. Why don't you give it a shot?"

He did. A short time later he came to me as a new man. His hair was cut and he was wearing a sharp suit. He had indeed gotten a job selling cars. He has been successful ever since. He and his family, who have since moved to another city, now have a car of their own and are buying their own house.

This young man was contained by a poverty mentality until his eyes were opened to greater possibilities. He broke out and has been free ever since. It is the grace of God that made this possible.

For one thing, this young man was already a Christian. He was already covered by God's grace. He simply was not aware of the potential that was inside him. Once he realized the creative power that God had given him, it made all the difference in the world to his outlook. For another thing, when I talked to him initially, I told him the story of the woman at the well and how Jesus had promised her that He could give her living water that would spring up into everlasting life. I explained to him that the living water of the Lord was the secret to his success. This living water is the grace of God, which covers us and makes all things possible for us as we live in Him.

Anointing. If the grace of God is the gift that makes all things possible for us, then the anointing of the Spirit is the power of God that makes the grace flow over us, through us, and out of us to touch others. Grace is the eternal resource; the anointing is the power that makes it happen. It is the free flow of the Spirit of God in our lives. The Bible says that the anointing breaks the yoke of bondage that causes containment: "It shall come to pass in that day that his burden will be taken away from your shoulder, and his yoke from your neck, and the yoke will be destroyed because of the anointing oil" (Is. 10:27).

The anointing is that active flow of the Spirit of God in your life that frees you to be and do your best in whatever you are doing. It is the unfettered movement of the Holy Spirit that achieves in you and through you the desire and heart of God. God yearns for you and others to be released into the "glorious liberty of the children of God" (Rom. 8:21b). He does not want you to be bound in any way. Paul encouraged the Galatians to "stand fast therefore in the liberty by which Christ has made us free, and do not be entangled again with a yoke of bondage" (Gal. 5:1).

So God's free grace is the resource that makes freedom a possibility for you, and the anointing is the power that brings about your freedom. Early in his Gospel John says, "But as many as received Him, to them gave He power to become the sons of God, even to them that believe on His name" (Jn. 1:12 KJV). You can't become a child of God unless He gives you the power to do so. The anointing is the power of God that makes you God's child.

Faith. The spiritual endowment that makes the grace and the anointing of God effective in our lives is faith. Ephesians 2:8 says that faith, like grace, is the gift of God. Faith is absolutely essential. It is critical. The writer of Hebrews says, "But without faith it is impossible to please Him, for he who comes to God must believe that He is, and that He is a rewarder of those who diligently seek Him" (Heb. 11:6). Without faith it is impossible to please God. No matter what we do or say, without faith it doesn't mean a thing.

On the other hand, all things are possible for him who has faith. Jesus told the father of a demon-possessed boy, "All things are possible to him who believes" (Mk. 9:23b). Once we gain the perspective of faith, all things, even the miraculous, become gloriously possible.

In simple terms, faith is believing in and acting on God's Word. Matthew and Mark both tell of the woman who had a hemorrhage for 12 years and who was healed when she touched the hem of Jesus' garment (see Mt. 9:20-22; Mk. 5:25-34). She had said to herself that if she could only touch Jesus' clothes, she would be healed. That was a faith statement. She knew that she would be made whole; all she needed to do was the necessary action to bring it about. That action was to press through the throng to get to Jesus. Despite the large crowd pressing around Him, when this woman touched Jesus, He instantly knew that healing power had gone out from Him. Jesus always knows and feels the pull of faith. It is like no other touch. For this woman, faith was critical. If she had not had the faith to reach out, she would not have received her healing.

Jesus said that if you have faith the size of a mustard seed, you can move mountains (see Mt. 17:20). That's how great faith is. While Jesus walked the earth He experienced the same human limitations that we do. The difference was that He operated in the realm of faith all the time. He had implicit, unshakable faith in His Father's will and purpose. That's why He was able to perform all the signs and wonders that He did.

You need to do more than simply *have* faith; you need to learn to *walk* by faith just as Jesus did. Otherwise you will never experience breakout. If you are to be effective in helping to release other people from containment, you must model faith before them and help them to exercise the faith they need in order to be set free. By His own laws and promises, God *always* responds to genuine faith. Whenever anyone says yes to God from the heart and not just the head, He responds with grace and mercy.

God has given you every resource you need to experience breakout. You have His power because you have His Spirit living in you. He has already defeated the enemy that tries to hold you back, and has armed you with the weapons necessary to make your victory personal. The gifts and spiritual endowments you have received from Him are not found in the world, and the world cannot understand them. They have been given to you so that you may move forward and break out to a new and higher plane of life and work in Christ's power. You have the power to break out of whatever is holding you back and to help others do the same. Don't let satan hold you hostage. Break out!

Chapter 9

Breakout Living

Breaking out is one thing; staying that way is another. Satan is wily, devious, and never-tiring. He won't let us off the hook if he gets even half a chance. The moment any of us begin to live carelessly or indifferently to the truth of the Word of God, we lay ourselves open to the danger of becoming contained again. In his first epistle Peter gave his readers a stern and wise warning that applies to us as well: "Be sober, be vigilant; because your adversary the devil walks about like a roaring lion, seeking whom he may devour. Resist him, steadfast in the faith..." (1 Pet. 5:8-9). We cannot afford to let down our guard.

That's where commitment comes in. We must be committed to a life of freedom, which means that we must live and obey daily what the Bible demands of us as free people of God. Breakout is neither automatic nor easy. Consistency in reading the Word of God, in praying, and in examining our hearts before the Lord is essential for all who choose to break out into the greater, higher, and fuller life that God has for us. The powers of darkness most certainly will oppose us every step of the way, but we are not ignorant of satan's schemes or bound by his power. This is why it is important for us both to recognize how and where we are contained and to know the resources that God has provided to give us victory. Satan may oppose us, but the greater truth is that we have Christ with us and in us to carry us through.

Paul said to the Ephesians, "And do not be drunk with wine, in which is dissipation; but be filled with the Spirit" (Eph. 5:18). The command "be filled" refers to a continuing, on-going process, not a one-time event. Another way to say it would be, "Keep on being filled with the Spirit." The Lord has promised that He will both fill you and keep you. Your experience of that promise is conditional upon your opening up to the continual filling and refilling of the Spirit of God. God will always do what He says He will do because He is not a man that He should lie (see Num. 23:19). You can depend on Him because He is committed to you. You in turn must be committed to Him.

You may be asking: How do I enter into this intimate walk with God that characterizes breakout living? How can I tell whether or not I am contained in some area or am in danger of becoming contained? How can I be sure of victory? You enter in by learning how to abide in Christ; you measure yourself by using Jesus' words and example as a standard; and you become confident of victory as you receive the daily assurance that you are inseparably united to your Lord.

Abide in Christ

Jesus taught His disciples about breakout living (which is just another way of saying *spiritual* living) by using the analogy of a vine, its branches, and the vinedresser. John recorded the teaching in chapter 15 of his Gospel:

> *I am the true vine, and My Father is the vinedresser. Every branch in Me that does not bear fruit He takes away; and every branch that bears fruit He prunes, that it may bear more fruit. You are already clean because of the word which I have spoken to you. Abide in Me, and I in you. As the branch cannot bear fruit of itself, unless it abides in the vine, neither can you, unless you abide in Me. I am the vine, you are the branches. He who abides in Me, and I in him, bears much fruit; for without Me you can do nothing. If anyone does not abide in Me, he is cast out as a branch and is withered; and they gather them and throw them into the fire, and they are burned. If you abide in Me, and My words abide in you, you will ask what you desire, and it shall be done for you. By this My Father is glorified, that you bear much fruit; so you will be My disciples. As the Father loved Me, I also have loved you; abide in My love. If you keep My commandments, you will abide in My love, just as I have kept My Father's commandments and abide in His love. These things I have spoken to*

you, that My joy may remain in you, and that your joy may be full (John 15:1-11).

Jesus is the vine, we are the branches, and God is the vinedresser. The sole purpose of a branch is to bear fruit. This is why unfruitful branches are taken away and fruitful branches are pruned. Pruning prepares the branches to bear more plentiful fruit of a better quality. Healthy, abundantly fruitful branches reflect well on the vinedresser who has tended them. Jesus said that His Father, the vinedresser, is glorified (reflected well upon) by our fruitfulness, which is also a proof to the world that we are Jesus' disciples.

A branch can bear fruit only as long as it remains connected to the vine because the life of the branch is in the vine. In the same manner, you cannot be a fruitful disciple (a breakout believer) unless you remain vitally connected to Jesus, living in union and fellowship with Him. Cast-off branches wither and die; they are good for nothing except to be burned. Apart from Him you can do nothing because the fruit you bear is not your own but His. Only when you are joined with Him in a vital, living relationship can you bear fruit—fruit that is His alone. Truly your life is in Jesus, not in yourself, and the fruit you bear, whether abundant or meager, reflects how closely you are linked to Him.

Jesus calls you to this life of union with Him with the words, "Abide in Me, and I in you." It is a mutual abiding, a true union. This is not as much a command, perhaps, as it is an invitation; not as much something you are to *do* as much as a state of rest you are to enjoy in Him. You are *saved* and *kept* by His grace. There is no striving or work on your part. Rather, Jesus is calling your attention to a condition that already exists for you if you are a believer. You are already joined to Him and therefore receive life from Him as naturally as the branch receives the life of the vine. Jesus wants you simply to recognize and accept the life and rest that are in Him.

As you learn to abide in Christ, your love for Him will grow deeper and stronger, creating a greater hunger for God's Word and a most intense desire for prayer. By the grace of God, I pray every night. I can't go to sleep without praying. Even before I became a Christian I prayed every night, having learned this from my mother. She had a tremendous influence on me and taught me to pray.

This habit of praying every night is of ernomous benefit. Can you imagine living with a woman as your wife and never talking to her, but expecting a happy marriage? Yet this is precisely what too many Christians do to God. Or what if I never told my wife that I love her? Yet this is the way we treat God.

God wants to communicate with you. He knows that you cannot do anything if you don't take time to fellowship with Him. Without the presence of God you cannot break out because often your areas of containment are the result of habits that you cannot naturally change. That's why Jesus said, "If you abide in Me, and My words abide in you, you will ask what you desire, and it shall be done for you."

When you are living in breakout, both Bible study and prayer take on a whole new meaning and sense of urgency that were formerly missing. Bible reading becomes such a joy that you can't get enough. Prayer becomes not a chore but a vital link with your most important friend, God Almighty, and an awesome privilege that allows you to be involved in what He is doing in you and in the world.

The greatest fruit of abiding in Christ is love. As your love for Jesus grows, your desire to obey Him will grow also. In fact, your obedience is proof of your love. When you abide in Christ in loving obedience, you know a fullness of joy that is far beyond any other joy. This joy comes not only from your obedience but also from the wondrous knowledge that God designed you to be in a vital, intimate union with Him and that He has reestablished that connection through the death of Jesus on the cross and the subsequent giving of the Holy Spirit to every believer. This is why Jesus said, "These things I have spoken to you, that My joy may remain in you, and that your joy may be full." Living with Jesus in a close, loving relationship brings joy.

You need not strive to get to this place of abiding in Christ; you are already there. God's grace has put you there and it keeps you there. Your part is to rest in Christ, being careful to avoid anything that would disrupt or hinder your abiding.

I have found over the years that the following practice works well for me to keep me abiding in Christ: When I start to get troubled in my mind, or I get anxious about work and people, I start thinking about all the lovely words like peace, joy, happiness, and love. I go through a whole list of anything that comes into my mind. This brings calm to my spirit and my soul because whatever impacts my thoughts impacts my life. If I can allow these things of Christ to change my thinking I have won the battle, since people basically do what they think. Or if I am troubled, I get up in the morning and repeat Psalm 23. "He restores my soul" (Ps. 23:3a). I love that. As I cling to His promise to restore my soul, He does just that, and I discover once again just how powerful His Word is. Truly abiding in Christ–allowing Him to influence my thoughts, words, and actions through His Word and His presence with me–is living that breaks me out of whatever problems, fears, or stresses I may be facing. This becomes particularly true as I meditate on the standards for daily living that Jesus taught during His earthly ministry and allow the Holy Spirit to quicken to my heart those words that will work change in me now, today.

Let Christ Be Your Standard

You see, my learning to recognize the signs and symptoms of containment is a necessary first step before I can effectively break out. I can't change unless I understand and accept the nature of my containment. The question is, How can I do that? How can I judge whether or not I am being contained–or am about to be contained–in some part of my life?

> The measure of your containment is directly related to how Christ-like or unChrist-like you are in your daily responses to the people, events, and circumstances of life.

Very simply: I measure my freedom or containment by the life of Jesus. To do this, I compare my attitudes, thoughts, and behavior in the midst of the everyday situations of my life to the example of Jesus' life and teaching. Jesus is my perfect example and my standard for living. He's yours too if you have taken Him as your Savior and Lord. Thus, the measure of your containment is directly related to how Christ-like or unChrist-like you are in your responses to the many people, events, and circumstances that are part of your daily life.

The four Gospels contain many teachings of Jesus that set the standard for us in our daily living. One passage that does this particularly well is found in chapter 6 of Luke. In a setting sometimes called His "Sermon on the Plain," Jesus gives instruction similar to and parallel with His Sermon on the Mount recorded in Matthew's Gospel. In both sets of teaching much emphasis is placed on our attitudes and behavior toward one another. Consider these words of Jesus:

> *But I say to you who hear: Love your enemies, do good to those who hate you, bless those who curse you, and pray for those who spitefully use you. To him who strikes you on the one cheek, offer the other also. And from him who takes away your cloak, do not withhold your tunic either. Give to everyone who asks of you. And from him who takes away your goods do not ask them back. And just as you want men to do to you, you also do to them likewise. But if you love those who love you, what credit is that to you? For even sinners love those who love them. And if you do good to those who do good to you, what credit is that to you? For even sinners do the same. And if you lend to those from whom you hope to receive back, what credit is that to you? For even sinners lend to sinners to receive as much back. But love your enemies, do good, and lend, hoping for nothing in return; and your reward will be great, and you will be sons of the Most High. For He is kind to the unthankful and evil. Therefore be merciful, just as your Father also is merciful* (Luke 6:27-36).

Even a casual reading of these verses reveals that Jesus is talking about a plane of living that few people ever attain. It is all but impossible to read this passage with an open mind and not become deeply convicted because we fall miles short of the standard Jesus sets here. Truly these guidelines show us just how contained we still are in many areas; there are many spiritual lessons we have yet to learn...or at least to consistently apply in our lives.

In verse 27 Jesus says, "I say to you who *hear*." There is more to this than simply hearing with the ear; it is listening to learn and understand what is meant. Verse 20 says that Jesus "lifted up His eyes toward His disciples." He is speaking to those who have committed themselves to follow Him and to obey His teachings. Jesus is surrounded by a multitude who had gathered to be healed and to witness miracles. Some came to hear His teaching, but most were concerned primarily with what Jesus could do for them. Jesus did heal those who came to Him and showed compassion on the crowd, but when it came time to teach, He addressed Himself primarily to those who would hear Him not with their ears alone but also with their spirits. Only those who had their hearts tuned to spiritual truth could receive the radical concepts He was about to present.

Love your enemies; do good to those who hate you. What an incredible thing to say! It goes completely against the grain of what the world says we should do. *Love your enemies?* Preposterous. *Do good to those who hate you?* That's crazy! Yet this is exactly what Jesus said to do. Isaiah 55:8 says that God's thoughts are not our thoughts; neither are His ways our ways. Jesus is calling us to a whole new way of thinking: God's way.

So you must ask yourself: Do I love my enemies? Do I do good to those who hate me, or do I feel vengeful and try to get even? How you respond to these questions reveals how contained you are in your attitudes and actions toward people who misuse you or in some way seek to harm you.

Bless those who curse you, and pray for those who spitefully use you. When was the last time you prayed specifically for someone who had spoken against you, had talked about you behind your back, or in some manner had sought to hurt you? Your level of containment or breakout can be measured by the depth and sincerity of your prayers for these people. Your *sincere* prayer for those who spitefully use you and say all manner of evil against you falsely is the undeniable evidence that you have broken through the wall of containment that hatred, resentment, and the desire for revenge puts around you. Freedom comes as you genuinely desire and pray for God's best for the person who has offended you. Impossible? Not at all. Nothing is impossible with God. Whatever Jesus tells you to do, He enables you to do.

To him who strikes you on the one cheek, offer the other also. This is a tough one. I am half Irish and if anybody strikes me on the cheek, my natural reaction is to push his teeth down his throat. In Matthew 5:9 Jesus said, "Blessed are the peacemakers, for they shall be called sons of God." Being a peacemaker means not only living peaceably with others, or mediating peace between those who are in disagreement, but also responding peaceably to others' aggressive actions against us. Turning the other cheek is not a passive avoidance of conflict. It is a *deliberate decision* to live in peace, a choice that requires courage and faith.

From him who takes away your cloak, do not withhold your tunic either. Is Jesus serious? If someone steals or demands my coat, am I supposed to give him my shirt as well? That's rather far-fetched, isn't it? No. It is Christ-like. True Christianity is living the way Jesus lives, not the way the world lives, and His Word is the standard by which you must judge your actions. The world's opinion does not matter. You are not of the world. Rather, your heart as a believer is to please God. You do this as you choose and continue in the way Jesus taught His followers to live. If all Christians did this, our churches would be filled to standing room only with people clamoring to find the life in Christ that we have.

Give to everyone who asks of you. And from him who takes away your goods do not ask them back. That goes against the grain too, doesn't it? We tend to be very possessive of our "goods." The world encourages that mentality. Only as you see yourself as a steward of God's bounty and regard your possessions as things He has entrusted into your keeping to be used and shared for His glory can you loosen the tight grip on things most Christians are inclined to have. When you are faithful with what God has provided, He continues to provide for you from His unlimited resources. Besides, as a child of God we are an heir to His Kingdom. All that belongs to Him (which is everything), He has given to His children. So examine your grip on your money and your possessions. What you discover will clearly reveal how contained or free you are in this area of life.

And just as you want men to do to you, you also do to them likewise. This is an active command. You are not simply to refrain from treating others the way you don't want to be treated, but are actively and deliberately to treat others the way you want to be treated...whether or not they treat you that way. In other words, anyone who observes your lifestyle should be able to see Christ—His person and teachings—in you.

Love your enemies, do good, and lend, hoping for nothing in return; and your reward will be great, and you will be sons of the Most High. For He is kind to the unthankful and evil. In verse 33 of Luke chapter 6, Jesus asks what credit it is to us if we love, do good for, and lend only to those who do the same for us. After all, even sinners do that. Your behavior as a believer must be of a higher standard. Jesus wants you to come to a place of relationship with Him where, like Him, you love the unlovely, the unkind, and the ungrateful.

Be merciful, just as your Father also is merciful. God hates sin but loves the sinner. He extends abundant mercy to those who ask in humility and repentance. His heart of mercy is toward the lost of this world, as is clearly revealed by Jesus' coming to us as a human being and dying on the cross for our sins that we might be saved.

The Scriptures clearly state that this mercy is given while we are still sinners: "But God demonstrates His own love toward us, in that while we were still sinners, Christ died for us" (Rom. 5:8). How can we then restrict our mercy to those who request it or deserve it? We can't. It is time we understand anew that we have been saved by the grace of God to serve. God's heart is burdened for the many people who are headed for hell because they have ignored Him or have outright rejected Him. He cares about the men, women, and children who have yet to hear the good news of Jesus.

These people are all around you. Satan would harden your heart toward them, or better yet give you an attitude of apathy or helplessness, but God calls you to share His burden and reach out to the lost as you follow your Lord and Savior. Apart from Jesus the lost are without hope. This was once your condition and mine. By the grace and mercy of God we have been saved through faith in Jesus Christ and have been delivered from sin's curse. Now we need to roll up our sleeves and be down-to-earth men and women of God who see the need and work to fill it.

If we do these things, we will break out. The devil most definitely will not be able to hold us back. Wherever we go, people will notice the difference in us and will give us opportunity to testify to the goodness of God in our lives. Then people will flock to receive a God who does such wonderful things for and through His people. That's the kind of God people are looking for, a God who makes a difference in daily life.

So be careful not to measure where you are in Christ or the level of freedom you have attained by what other people say, think, or do. You cannot judge yourself by comparing yourself to another person—no matter how much you may respect that person as a powerful saint of God. Rather, you must use the word and example of Jesus as the standard against which you evaluate and judge your heart and your daily performance. Only as you live according to what He expects of you can you find freedom and fulfillment. Remember, God never expects the impossible of you. He only asks that you trust Him, obey Him, and allow Him to work the impossible in and through you. This breakout living happens as you allow the life, the mind, and the heart of Christ to be formed in you.

Nothing Can Separate Us

Breakout living requires courage, faith, and vision: courage to challenge the obstacles between where you are and the higher plane of life you are pursuing; faith to follow God's leading even when circumstances dictate a different course; and vision to see God's plan for you and others and allow it to inspire you to reach for the prize no matter what the cost. Sometimes the road is rough and steep, and the journey is tiring. You may even feel like quitting at times.

Life will not always be so. God has promised you the leveling or moving of mountains and an abundance of joy in the journey. Take Him at His Word. Find in Him the strength for the journey. You'll not be sorry. Why? His very presence will sustain you, and His right hand will uphold you: "You have also given me the shield of Your salvation; Your right hand has held me up, Your gentleness has made me great. You enlarged my path under me, so my feet did not slip" (Ps. 18:35-36.) Above all you can rely on this promise: "I will never leave you nor forsake you" (Heb. 13:5c).

Whatever way you walk, Jesus has walked it before you (see Heb. 4:15); whichever way you turn, He is there to light the way (see Jn. 8:12). There is nowhere you can go that He is not there; His presence is with you always (see Ps. 139:7-10). Truly nothing can separate you from God and His love for you. Paul wonderfully testified to this glorious truth in chapter 8 of Romans:

> *And we know that all things work together for good to those who love God, to those who are the called according to His purpose. For whom He foreknew, He also predestined to be conformed to the image of His Son, that He might be the firstborn among many brethren. Moreover whom He predestined, these He also called; whom He called, these He also justified; and whom He justified, these He also glorified. What then shall we say to these things? If God is for us, who can be against us? He who did not spare His own Son, but delivered Him up for us all, how shall He not with Him also freely give us all things?...Who shall separate us from the love of Christ? Shall tribulation, or distress, or persecution, or famine, or nakedness, or peril, or sword?...Yet in all these things we are more than conquerors through Him who loved us. For I am persuaded that neither death nor life, nor angels nor principalities nor powers, nor things present nor things to come, nor height nor depth, nor any other created thing, shall be able to*

separate us from the love of God which is in Christ Jesus our Lord (Romans 8:28-32,35,37-39).

You are not alone on your journey. God is with you, calling you on into all that He has planned for your life and giving you the strength to take the next step. His promise still stands: *All things work together for good to those who love God.* When you walk with the Lord, nothing touches you that does not first pass through Him. He is your strength, your refuge, your stronghold, and your protector. Because He loves you and has a marvelous plan for you, He can turn whatever happens in your life–good or bad–to serve His purpose concerning you.

You may say, "What is God's purpose for my life? I'm not sure I understand that." More than anything else, God wants you to be "conformed to the image of His Son." This is the definition of breakout living. Conforming involves shaping and molding, neither of which come without some pain and discomfort. Nevertheless, God is shaping your "earthen vessel" into a glorious container fit for His use. By fitting you for service on earth, He is preparing you to reign with Him in Heaven.

If God is for us, who can be against us? With the God of the universe on our side, how can we lose? More accurately, when *we* choose to be on *God's* side, we have chosen certain victory. We can only choose Him because He first chose us. Paul said that God chose us in Christ "before the foundation of the world, that we should be holy and without blame before Him in love, having predestined us to adoption as sons by Jesus Christ to Himself, according to the good pleasure of His will" (Eph. 1:4b-5).

In other words, God chose you because He wanted to! He confirmed His choice by sending Jesus to die for you. How could you fail or want for anything with a God who gave up for your sake that which was most precious to Him, His own Son?

Who shall separate us from the love of Christ? As believers we have been joined to Jesus Christ in an eternal, inseparable union just as branches are joined to the vine. As we abide in Christ we abide in His love, which is everlasting. God said, "I have loved you with an everlasting love; therefore with lovingkindness I have drawn you" (Jer. 31:3b).

Nothing that you face now, and nothing that will come against you in the future in either the natural realm or the supernatural realm, will ever be able to separate you from the love of God that has drawn you to Him in Christ Jesus. God has purposed to make you perfect and complete in His Son; and what He has started, He will finish. Paul told the Philippians, "He who has begun a good work in you will complete it until the day of Jesus Christ" (Phil. 1:6b).

Breakout living means believing the promises of God concerning you, stepping out in faith to claim them, and moving forward to bring the whole world to the knowledge of God's love in Jesus Christ—being confident of certain victory.

Dear friend, your sinful, shameful past—your "old man"—is dead and gone, nailed to the cross with Jesus. Your future is secure in Christ and is as bright as the promises of God. What remains to be seen is what you will do with the here and now—with each new day, which is the gift of God. Are you living in the fullness of God's intent for your life? Are you reaching toward your highest potential in life and ministry? Do you rest in the abiding place with Jesus? Are you "press[ing] toward the goal for the prize of the upward call of God in Christ Jesus" (Phil. 3:14)?

I pray that you are. Indeed, my challenge for each of you is this: Tear down the walls that contain you! Break through the barriers that hold you back from God's best! Stop allowing your life to be determined by the lies of satan and the negative and corrupt ideas and values of the world. Let containment go. Take God at His word and break out! He has already given you everything you need to enjoy an abundant, victorious, and totally fulfilling life. Glory to God! Hallelujah!

Check out these books from Destiny Image that will help you release the spirit within!

hen your heart is yearning for more of Jesus, these books by Don Nori will help!

NO MORE SOUR GRAPES

Who among us wants our children to be free from the struggles we have had to bear? Who among us wants the lives of our children to be full of victory and love for their Lord? Who among us wants the hard-earned lessons from our lives given freely to our children? All these are not only possible, they are also God's will. You can be one of those who share the excitement and joy of seeing your children step into the destiny God has for them. If you answered "yes" to these questions, the pages of this book are full of hope and help for you and others just like you.
ISBN 0-7684-2037-7

THE POWER OF BROKENNESS

Accepting Brokenness is a must for becoming a true vessel of the Lord, and is a stepping-stone to revival in our hearts, our homes, and our churches. Brokenness alone brings us to the wonderful revelation of how deep and great our Lord's mercy really is. Join this companion who leads us through the darkest of nights. Discover the *Power of Brokenness*.
ISBN 1-56043-178-4

THE ANGEL AND THE JUDGMENT

Few understand the power of our judgments—or the aftermath of the words we speak in thoughtless, emotional pain. In this powerful story about a preacher and an angel, you'll see how the heavens respond and how the earth is changed by the words we utter in secret.
ISBN 1-56043-154-7

HIS MANIFEST PRESENCE

This is a passionate look at God's desire for a people with whom He can have intimate fellowship. Not simply a book on worship, it faces our triumphs as well as our sorrows in relation to God's plan for a dwelling place that is splendid in holiness and love.
ISBN 0-914903-48-9
Also available in Spanish.
ISBN 1-56043-079-6

SECRETS OF THE MOST HOLY PLACE

Here is a prophetic parable you will read again and again. The winds of God are blowing, drawing you to His Life within the Veil of the Most Holy Place. There you begin to see as you experience a depth of relationship your heart has yearned for. This book is a living, dynamic experience with God!
ISBN 1-56043-076-1

HOW TO FIND GOD'S LOVE

Here is a heartwarming story about three people who tell their stories of tragedy, fear, and disease, and how God showed them His love in a real way.
ISBN 0-914903-28-4
Also available in Spanish.
ISBN 1-56043-024-9

Available at your local Christian bookstore.

Internet: http://www.reapernet.com

B6:102

The Lord wants His power flowing through all of us in the everyday experience of our lives. Read about His purposes for all of us in these books!

GOD CAN USE LITTLE OLE ME

by Randy Clark.

Do you believe that God uses only the educated, the dynamic, and the strong in faith to do the work of His Kingdom? Be prepared to be surprised! In this practical, down-to-earth book, Randy Clark shows that God uses ordinary people, often in extraordinary ways, to accomplish His purposes. Through his own personal experience and the testimonies of other "little ole me's," Randy shows that God still heals today, and that He is using everyday Christians to be involved with Him in a healing ministry to the world.

ISBN 1-56043-696-4

EXTRAORDINARY POWER FOR ORDINARY CHRISTIANS

by Erik Tammaru.

Ordinary people don't think too much about extraordinary power. We think that this kind of power is for extraordinary people. We forget that it is this supernatural power that makes us all extraordinary! We are all special in His sight and we all have the hope of extraordinary living. His power can change ordinary lives into lives empowered by the Holy Spirit and directed by His personal love for us.

ISBN 1-56043-309-4

A HEART FOR GOD

by Charles P. Schmitt.

This powerful book will send you on a 31-day journey with David from brokenness to wholeness. Few men come to God with as many millstones around their necks as David did. Nevertheless, David pressed beyond adversity, sin, and failure into the very forgiveness and deliverance of God. The life of David will bring hope to those bound by generational curses, those born in sin, and those raised in shame. David's life will inspire faith in the hearts of the dysfunctional, the failure-ridden, and the fallen!

ISBN 1-56043-157-1

RELEASERS OF LIFE

by Mary Audrey Raycroft.

Inside you is a river that is waiting to be tapped—the river of the Holy Spirit and power! Let Mary Audrey Raycroft, a gifted exhorter and teacher and the Pastor of Equipping Ministries and Women in Ministry at the Toronto Airport Christian Fellowship, teach you how you can release the unique gifts and anointings that the Lord has placed within you. Discover how you can move and minister in God's freeing power and be a releaser of life!

ISBN 1-56043-198-9

Available at your local Christian bookstore.

Internet: http://www.reapernet.com

Other Destiny Image titles
you will enjoy reading

CORPORATE ANOINTING
by Kelley Varner.
Just as a united front is more powerful in battle, so is the anointing when Christians come together in unity! In this classic book, senior pastor Kelley Varner of Praise Tabernacle in Richlands, North Carolina, presents a powerful teaching and revelation that will change your life! Learn how God longs to reveal the fullness of Christ in the fullness of His Body in power and glory.
ISBN 0-7684-2011-3

PERCEIVING THE WHEEL OF GOD
by Dr. Mark Hanby.
On the potter's wheel, a lump of clay yields to a necessary process of careful pressure and constant twisting. Similarly, the form of true faith is shaped by a trusting response to the hand of God in a suffering situation. This book offers essential understanding for victory through the struggles of life.
ISBN 1-56043-109-1

THE LOST ART OF INTERCESSION
by Jim W. Goll.
Finally there is something that really explains what is happening to so many folk in the Body of Christ. What does it mean to carry the burden of the Lord? Where is it in Scripture and in history? Why do I feel as though God is groaning within me? No, you are not crazy; God is restoring genuine intercessory prayer in the hearts of those who are open to respond to His burden and His passion.
ISBN 1-56043-697-2

DIGGING THE WELLS OF REVIVAL
by Lou Engle.
Did you know that just beneath your feet are deep wells of revival? God is calling us today to unstop the wells and reclaim the spiritual inheritance of our nation, declares Lou Engle. As part of the pastoral staff at Harvest Rock Church and founder of its "24-Hour House of Prayer," he has experienced firsthand the importance of knowing and praying over our spiritual heritage. Let's renew covenant with God, reclaim our glorious roots, and believe for the greatest revival the world has ever known!
ISBN 0-7684-2015-6

Available at your local Christian bookstore.

Internet: http://www.reapernet.com

B6:105